Macbeth

edited by

Roma Gill
M.A. *Cantab*. B.Litt. *Oxon*.
Senior Lecturer in English Literature
University of Sheffield

Oxford University Press

Oxford University Press, Walton Street, Oxford OX2 6DP

London New York Toronto
Delhi Bombay Calcutta Madras Karachi
Kuala Lumpur Singapore Hong Kong Tokyo
Nairobi Dar es Salaam Cape Town
Melbourne Auckland

and associated companies in
Beirut Berlin Ibadan Mexico City Nicosia

Oxford is a trade mark of Oxford University Press

First published 1977
Reprinted 1978, 1980, 1981 (twice), 1982, 1983, 1984 (twice)

For Mandy

Oxford School Shakespeare
edited by Roma Gill

A Midsummer Night's Dream
Romeo and Juliet
As You Like It
Macbeth
Julius Caesar
The Merchant of Venice
Henry IV Part I

Printed in Great Britain
at the University Press, Oxford

A letter to all students of this text

I want to say a few words of explanation to all those readers who are studying this text for examination purposes. I'm sure that Shakespeare would be very pleased with the kind of attention that you and I are going to give to the words of his play—but he would also be very surprised. He wrote his plays to be *acted*. He did not think that they would be *read*—and read more than 300 years after he had written them. He cared so little for *readers*, that many of his plays were not printed until after his death.

Act this play! Enjoy the characters, the situations, and the language. Don't worry too much if you don't fully understand the language at first. A modern poet, T. S. Eliot, has said that the best poetry will mean *something* to the reader before it is completely understood.

Shakespeare wrote the best poetry; but his language is not easy to appreciate, even for those who are native speakers of English. There are three reasons for this.

Firstly, you will find that some words look odd because there is an apostrophe where you would expect a letter: the word 'ever', for instance, often appears as 'e'er'. Many verbs appear in the past tense as (for example) 'look'd', which you have been properly taught to spell 'looked'. This is because of the length of Shakespeare's verse line which has ten syllables (when it is regular). By writing 'e'er' and not 'ever' the dramatist managed to save one syllable. It is almost the same with verbs in the past tense. Although today 'looked' is pronounced as one syllable, in Shakespeare's time it could have been two—'look-ed'. The spelling 'look'd' instructs you to use a modern English pronunciation. When you find 'looked' in poetry, you should pronounce the second syllable as well as the first. This care for the rhythm of the lines is not needed in the prose parts of the play, and so the spelling there is the spelling of modern English.

The second problem is that we no longer speak the English of Shakespeare's time. Many words have changed their meaning. When Caithness calls Malcolm 'the medicine of the sickly weal' (*Macbeth*, 5, 2, 27) we need to be told that 'medicine' here means 'doctor' and that 'weal' (a poetic form of 'wealth') means 'land' or 'country'. Caithness is saying that Malcolm (who is the rightful king of Scotland) will be able to put right the country's troubles.

Finally, it is sometimes hard to understand what a character is saying. This is because Shakespeare had a very powerful mind, and his thoughts are not always easy to understand. As well as this, he liked to play with words, as we see when Macbeth murmurs to himself

> If it were done when 'tis done, then 'twere well
> It were done quickly.   (*1*, 8, 1–2)

Macbeth is thinking of murdering his king, and he plays with the different meanings of the word 'done'. He is saying that if the business of the murder was *ended* ('done') as soon as it was *performed* ('done'), then it would be a good thing that it should be *carried out* ('done') as soon as possible. In the rest of the play Shakespeare shows us that the murder was not completed when the king died, but that Macbeth was forced to kill more people in order to hide his first crime. At the same time, he had to recognize his guilt, and bear his punishment.

Don't think a lot about the past. It is true that Shakespeare was writing in the sixteenth and early seventeenth centuries, as you will see from the Table on p. 95. Yet soon after his death Ben Jonson, who was a friend of Shakespeare's and a playwright himself, said of him that 'He was not of an age, but for all time'. The characters that Shakespeare has created, and the feelings that he has described, are alive in *our* world. You must know of girls who are in love, of men who are politically ambitious, and of misers who only care about money. These, and many more, are the characters in Shakespeare's plays.

Study this play then; and act it. Read it aloud. You owe it to yourselves and to your teachers to do as well as you can in the examinations. You also have a debt to Shakespeare, and you can pay this debt by *acting* the play, and enjoying it—just as he intended it to be acted, and enjoyed. You need no fancy costumes or expensive scenery. Shakespeare's own professional actors had very little scenery. Their clothes had often been given to them by rich courtiers who were tired of them. There were no women among these actors, for it was not thought respectable for a woman to act. Boys played the parts of the female characters.

This play is given to you as it would be given to a company of actors. You are told when each character comes on to the stage ('*Enter* Macbeth'), and when he leaves ('*Exit*'). It is traditional in the theatre to use Latin here, saying 'exit' for 'he goes out', or 'exeunt' for 'they go out'. Sometimes you will find a stage direction telling you that a noise is heard 'within'. This simply means that the noise is off-stage. Very often a scene is introduced with music, or with the sound of trumpets if a king is to enter. This music is like the soundtrack of a film: it helps the audience to find the proper mood for the action.

In the Introduction and the Notes I have tried to help you as much as I can. But I may well have missed something that you could tell me about. If this happens, please write to me at the local office of the Oxford University Press. Your letters will be forwarded to me, and I shall be very happy to hear from you.

Roma Gill

Contents

Macbeth: A play for the king   ix

Leading characters in the play   xi

Macbeth: The play   xiii

Macbeth: The man   xxiv

Characters in the play   xxviii

Macbeth   I

Examinations   87

William Shakespeare: life and works   93

Macbeth: A play for the king

When Elizabeth I of England was dying, childless, she named James VI of Scotland as her successor. He became James I of England.

In August 1606 James was at Hampton Court, a palace near London, entertaining his brother-in-law, King Christian of Denmark. A play was acted for them, *Macbeth*, written by the best dramatist of the time, William Shakespeare. It was a new play, but the story was an old one. James knew it well, because it was about ancestors, Banquo and Fleance, through whom he had inherited the throne of Scotland.

Shakespeare found the story in *The History of Scotland*, by Raphael Holinshed, but his play is much more than a dramatic re-writing of the historical facts. He made many changes, and the biggest of these concerned James's ancestor. In the true story, Banquo joined Macbeth in killing Duncan; but clearly it would be tactless to suggest that James was descended from a regicide—the murderer of a king. So Shakespeare's Banquo is innocent.

James also believed that he was descended spiritually from the long tradition of English monarchs, and that he had inherited the power of healing that Edward the Confessor (1042–66) possessed. Shakespeare's description of this power (4, 3, 146–56) is, to some extent, deliberate flattery of his king. Shakespeare also knew that James was extremely interested in witchcraft, and had written a book about it.

Macbeth is certainly a play 'fit for a king'.

But of course it is more than this—more than flattery for an ancient British monarch; and although the story is largely true, we do not read *Macbeth* as 'history'. We could interpret Shakespeare's play as a moral lesson. Macbeth murders his king. To murder any man is a crime, but those who lived at the time of Shakespeare thought that the murder of a *king* was the greatest of all crimes. Kings were appointed by God, to rule as His deputies: rebellion against a true king was rebellion against God. By murdering Duncan, Macbeth gains the crown; but he loses love, friendship, respect—and in the end his life. His crime is rightly punished.

There is still more to the play. On one 'level' it is royal entertainment—and entertainment, too, for all those of us who enjoy the suspense and excitement of a murder story. On another level, it teaches us, in a new way, the old lesson that crime does not pay. But there are two more levels.

As we look at the character of Macbeth we see, more clearly than we are able to see in real life, the effects of uncontrolled ambition on a man who is, except for his ambition, noble in nature. Macbeth has full knowledge of right and wrong; he knows that he has committed a very great crime by murdering Duncan. Shakespeare shows us how Macbeth becomes hardened to his crimes, and yet how he suffers from fears which he has created himself.

On the last level, the play has great power as a work of poetry and imagination. The language is rich in sound and meaning, full of pictures, and immensely varied. Take this episode, for example. When Macbeth comes from the murder of Duncan, his hands are covered in the king's blood; he looks at them, and feels that all the waters in the ocean cannot wash away the blood, but that

> this my hand will rather
> The multitudinous seas incarnadine,
> Making the green one red.   (2, 2, 61–3)

The word 'multitudinous' gives a sense of vastness, and 'incarnadine' (meaning 'redden') is another impressive word; its length and sound give strength to the meaning. The two words are more Latin than English, and were very new to the English language; Shakespeare was one of the first writers to use them. They are followed by the simplest, most direct words. Imagine a film camera. First the camera shows you a picture of endless waters, stretching as far as the eye can see: then a sudden close-up picture, perhaps a small pool of green water that turns red with blood as we look at it. Such skill in the use of language is unique.

Although I have distinguished four levels on which the play *Macbeth* can work, I do not want to give the impression that these levels can in fact be separated from each other. The entertainment, the moral teaching, the psychology, and the poetry are often all contained in the same speech—even, sometimes, in the same line. *Macbeth* demands an alert reader.

No summary can do justice to the play. At best, a commentary such as this can be no more than a map. It can show the roads, and even point out the important places; but it is no substitute for reading the play.

Leading characters in the play

Duncan The king of Scotland, murdered by Macbeth. Duncan is a true and gracious king, who represents the Elizabethan concept that the king was appointed by God, and is therefore almost divine.

Malcolm Duncan's elder son. Early in the play Malcolm is named as the next king of Scotland. After Duncan's murder Malcolm, with his brother Donalbain, escapes from Scotland. He takes refuge in England, at the court of Edward the Confessor, until he is able to lead an army against Macbeth. At the end of the play he is crowned king of Scotland.

Macbeth A mighty and ambitious warrior, one of the leaders of Duncan's army. He hears a prophecy that he will be king one day. This makes him more ambitious and leads him to murder Duncan. He is elected king of Scotland, but he becomes a cruel and unjust ruler. He is always conscious of guilt, and never knows a moment's peace after he has killed Duncan. At the end of the play he is killed by Macduff. (See also p. xxxiii.)

Lady Macbeth She is even more ambitious than her husband, and has no regard for morality. She urges Macbeth to kill Duncan, and refuses to understand his doubts and hesitations. Husband and wife are at first affectionate, hiding nothing from each other; gradually this relationship is destroyed. Lady Macbeth becomes obsessed with the murder of Duncan, suffers from nightmares, and finally kills herself.

Banquo He and Macbeth are the leaders of Duncan's army, but he is not so conspicuously valiant as Macbeth. It is prophesied that his children will be kings, but although he hopes that this prophecy will come true, he takes no action. He is killed by murderers working for Macbeth, but his son, Fleance, escapes.

Macduff A Scottish thane (nobleman), who comes to prominence after the murder of Duncan. Macbeth is particularly afraid of him, and orders murderers to kill Lady Macduff and her children. Macduff persuades Malcolm to lead an army against Macbeth, and it is he who kills Macbeth.

Ross   Although Ross has a large part in the play, he does not really have a 'character'. He brings messages, describes events, warns of dangers to come, and comments on the progress of the play.

Macbeth: The play

Act 1

Scene 1   A very short scene opens the play. It is long enough to awaken curiosity, but not to satisfy it. We have come in at the *end* of the witches' meeting, just as they are arranging their next appointment before their 'familiar spirits'—devils in animal shapes—call them away into the 'fog and filthy air'. The mood of the play is set here, although the action does not start until the next scene. Here we

Scene 2   learn about the tough battle, about the rebels who seem to have all the luck, and about two brave men, Macbeth and Banquo, who win the victory for Scotland. Duncan rewards Macbeth for his courage by giving him the title 'thane of Cawdor'; but we ought to remember that the title first belonged to one who was 'a most disloyal traitor'.

Scene 3   The witches' malice and magic are shown, as they await Macbeth on the lonely moor (a wasteland area). They have power over the winds, and can make life miserable for such men as the captain of the ship, 'The Tiger'. Their dance, when they hear Macbeth's drum, is made up of steps in groups of three— the magical number. Macbeth and Banquo, however, are ordinary human beings, tired after the day's fighting and grumbling about the weather. Banquo is almost amused by the witches; he cannot bring himself to think of them as women because 'your beards forbid me to interpret / That you are so'. Macbeth is stunned to silence by their prophecies, but Banquo questions them calmly.

The audience can judge the witches better than Macbeth can; *we* know, from the previous scene, that his courage, and not the witches' magic, has won him the title 'thane of Cawdor'; and we are not surprised, as he is, when Ross calls him by this title. While Ross, Angus, and Banquo speak together (perhaps at the back of the stage), Macbeth speaks his own thoughts aloud in a soliloquy— a speech not intended by the speaker to be overheard. They are frightening thoughts: they frighten Macbeth as well as us, for murder is in his mind. He tries to reject this first impulse, declaring that he will leave everything to chance:

> If chance will have me king, why, chance may crown me
> Without my stir.

Scene 4   When Duncan hears of the death of the treacherous thane of Cawdor, he utters a very meaningful remark:

> There's no art
> To find the mind's construction in the face.
> He was a gentleman on whom I built
> An absolute trust.

We have not seen the traitor, so we do not know how appropriate these words are for *him*; but we have seen his successor, and Macbeth is certainly a gentleman on whom Duncan is building 'An absolute trust'. Duncan's comment could also be applied to other persons and happenings in this play, where things are not what they seem to be, where 'Fair is foul and foul is fair'.

Duncan now makes a very important announcement:

> We will establish our estate upon
> Our eldest, Malcolm, whom we name hereafter
> The Prince of Cumberland.

In the time of Duncan the crown of Scotland was not passed automatically from father to son. Instead, the king could name his successor, as Duncan does here, and grant him the title 'Prince of Cumberland'. If the king were to die without naming an heir, or if the heir was not acceptable, the Scottish nobles could elect a new king. We hear that Macbeth is thus elected in *Act 2*, Scene 4. Duncan's choice comes as a great shock to Macbeth, for he recognizes it as an obstacle standing between him and the crown. At the end of the scene he admits to possessing 'black and deep desires', but he is afraid to speak these openly, even to himself.

Scene 5   We already know the contents of Macbeth's letter to his wife; but the letter is important because it shows us something of the relationship between Macbeth and Lady Macbeth: he has no secrets from her, and she is his 'dearest partner of greatness'. Lady Macbeth understands her husband well. She knows that he has great ambitions, but she also knows that he is honourable, and that this sense of honour will not allow him to 'catch the nearest way'. She knows that she will have to urge her husband on to become king, and she calls for evil spirits to help her. She will give up all the gentle, tender qualities of a woman, so that she can become a sexless, pitiless fiend. She takes full control over the situation, and Macbeth seems glad to let her have the responsibility.

Scene 7   Alone after dinner, Macbeth has the opportunity to think about the murder of his king, perhaps for the first time. At first murder had been only a dream, 'but fantastical' (*1*, 3, 139), but now it is a real moral problem. He knows that the crime must be punished; divine justice in a 'life to come' does not worry him so much as judgement in this earthly life. Then he considers the duties he owes to Duncan—the duties of a kinsman, of a subject to his king, and of a host to his guest. Finally he thinks of the character of Duncan, a king of almost divine excellence.

    Macbeth has a vision of the heavenly powers, horrified by this murder; he sees Pity, personified as a 'naked new-born babe' which is nevertheless 'Striding the blast', while 'heaven's cherubin' are mounted on the winds. The speech builds to a mighty climax— then suddenly the power is lost, when Macbeth turns to his own wretched motive for committing such a crime. He can find nothing except 'Vaulting ambition', and even now he realizes that too high a leap ('vault') can only lead to a fall.

    His mind is made up, and he tells his wife 'We will proceed no further in this business'. He is not prepared for her rage and abuse. She calls him a coward, insults his virility, and declares that she would have murdered her child while it was feeding at her breast, rather than break such a promise as Macbeth has done. Defeated by his wife's scorn, and persuaded by her encouragement, Macbeth agrees to murder his king.

Act 2

Scene 1   The witches have disturbed Banquo, as well as Macbeth. As he crosses the courtyard of Macbeth's castle he hears a noise, and calls for his sword: this suggests tension, for he should not need a sword in a friend's home. Macbeth also shows signs of stress, for he speaks few words in his replies to Banquo; and when he is alone, the strain shows very clearly. He is living in a nightmare, but although he is at first alarmed by the dagger that his imagination creates, he seems later to *enjoy* the horror of the moment. The last lines of the scene could even show a grim humour:

> the bell invites me.
> Hear it not, Duncan; for it is a knell
> That summons thee to heaven, or to hell.

Scene 2   Lady Macbeth is as tense as her husband, and she has been drinking to give herself courage. Her speech is jerky, for she reacts to every sound, and when her husband comes from the king's room, his hands red with Duncan's blood, she greets him with relief and pride: 'My husband'. He has now proved himself, in her eyes, to be a man. Macbeth slowly awakens from the nightmare he has been living in and realizes what a terrible crime he has committed. He speaks of the real sounds he has heard, and then of the voice that cried

> 'Sleep no more!
> Macbeth does murder sleep'

This ban will be carried out: never again will Macbeth, or his wife, have any rest, and from time to time throughout the play they will comment on their weariness and lack of refreshing sleep.

For the present, however, Lady Macbeth again takes charge of the situation. Early in this scene she revealed some natural, womanly feelings when she confessed that she could not murder Duncan herself because he 'resembled / My father as he slept'. But now she speaks a line which shows, terrifyingly, how little she thinks of the guilt that she shares with her husband:

> A little water clears us of this deed.

Scene 3   The mood of the play suddenly changes. The audience has been as tense as Macbeth and Lady Macbeth in the last scene, and we need to relax a little now. The Porter, woken from a drunken sleep, gives us something to laugh at. His jokes are not so funny today as they were in 1606, when his chatter about the 'equivocator' might have reminded the audience of the recent and notorious trial of a priest who could 'swear in both the scales against either scale'; but the wise observations on drink and lechery are still amusing.

Macduff and Lennox come almost from another world; or perhaps the Porter is more accurate than he thinks when he pretends to be porter at the gate of hell. The tension mounts again as we wait for the murder to be discovered.

Lennox's description of the 'unruly' night would have been full of significance to the Elizabethans. They firmly believed that any disorder in human affairs was reflected by disorder in the world of nature. Macbeth is cautious, but we cannot miss the understatement of his reply to Lennox: ''twas a rough night'.

The moment we have been waiting for arrives. Macduff's words emphasize the fact that this is more than an ordinary murder:

> Confusion now has made his masterpiece!
> Most sacrilegious murder hath broke ope
> The Lord's anointed temple.

The scene is chaotic: alarm-bells ring, and characters appear from all sides of the stage. Macduff is almost hysterical; the king's sons are afraid; Macbeth impulsively kills Duncan's servants—and by doing so arouses Macduff's suspicion. The speech in which Macbeth attempts to justify himself may perhaps convince the other thanes; but we know how false it is, and the elaborate images (for example, 'His silver skin lac'd with his golden blood') stress this falsehood. Lady Macbeth knows the truth too, for she faints (or pretends to faint) and some attention is drawn away from her husband.

Scene 4   The short scene between Ross and the Old Man serves three purposes. At first it continues the comparison begun in Lennox's lines in Scene 3 between the human world and the natural world, mentioning strange events and stressing that they are

> unnatural,
> Even like the deed that's done.

The second function of the scene appears when Macduff enters to bring more news: it indicates the passing of time. Thirdly, it brings Macduff into greater prominence, because it allows the actor playing the part of Macduff to reveal, by the tone of his voice, that Macduff continues to be suspicious of Macbeth, and that he does not himself believe the answers he gives to Ross's questions.

Act 3

Scene 1   Banquo also is suspicious of Macbeth:

> Thou hast it now: King, Cawdor, Glamis, all,
> As the weird women promis'd; and, I fear,
> Thou play'dst most foully for 't.

But he thinks about the prophecy concerning his own children, and this gives him hope. Macbeth too has been thinking about this prophecy, and it gives him cause for bitterness: he realizes that his crown is 'fruitless', and his sceptre 'barren' (see illustration, p. 65). He murdered Duncan in order to make the witches' prophecy come true, but now he plots to murder Banquo and Fleance so that the witches' promise to Banquo may *not* come true.

Scene 2   Lady Macbeth now begins to show signs of strain, and we hear that Macbeth suffers 'terrible dreams'. For a moment Macbeth and his wife show understanding and sympathy for each other, but the moment does not last long. Macbeth keeps secret from his wife the plot to murder Banquo. He alarms her by conjuring up an atmosphere of evil, and once again he appears to enjoy his dreadful imaginings (just as he did when he went to murder Duncan). But it is a mistake to hide the facts from Lady Macbeth: this is the beginning of the break in their relationship.

When Macbeth calls upon 'seeling night' to hide his wickedness, we remember how Lady Macbeth, before the murder of Duncan, had called for the night, shrouded in 'the dunnest smoke of hell' (*1*, 5, 50), to hide the murdering dagger from the sight of heaven.

Scene 3   Outside the castle, the two murderers wait for Banquo and Fleance. It is a surprise, to us as well as to them, when a third hired assassin appears. Macbeth can trust no-one, not even the thugs he first appointed to murder Banquo.

Scene 4   The confusion of Banquo's murder contrasts well with the ceremony of the state banquet. The formality is announced in the first line: 'You know your own degrees; sit down'; and the scene proceeds with dignity for some time. The appearance of one of Banquo's murderers disturbs the peace for Macbeth. The state occasion demands courteous behaviour from the king, but when the murderer says that Fleance has escaped, Macbeth is agitated. Banquo's Ghost, which only Macbeth can see, adds to this distress, until the whole scene breaks into fragments, and Lady Macbeth has to ask her guests to leave, without any of the formality with which they arrived:

> Stand not upon the order of your going,
> But go at once.

The banquet is symbolic as well as realistic, and Shakespeare is careful that we do not overlook this aspect. As soon as the guests are seated, Macbeth promises to 'drink a measure / The table round'. In many societies and religions, the sharing of a cup of wine, sometimes even called a 'loving-cup', symbolizes unity and fellowship; and so it is intended here. When Macbeth has stepped away from the table to speak to the murderer, Lady Macbeth calls him back, and reminds him of his duty as a host, adding that on such an occasion 'the sauce to meat is ceremony'. Macbeth brings chaos to Scotland, breaking up the harmony of a well-ordered country, just as he breaks up the state banquet 'With most admir'd disorder'.

Scene 5 It is a pity that this silly little scene has to be included in *Macbeth*. Shakespeare never wrote like this, and it was probably inserted into the play by some over-enthusiastic actor, who saw that the audiences enjoyed the witches' scenes, and decided to give them another. Or perhaps it is the work of an actor who found he had no part in the play, and so created the character of Hecate for himself, writing these lines, and five more in *Act 4*, Scene 1 (39–43). This person must also, I think, take the responsibility for the placing of Scene 6. This would be more appropriate coming *after* the visit to the witches, which should follow immediately after the banquet scene: Macbeth said then that he would call upon the witches 'tomorrow—And betimes I will', and he would not have postponed such an important errand.

Scene 6 Suspicion of Macbeth is growing. Lennox speaks here not as himself, an individual character, but with what we now call 'the voice of the people'. His words are innocent in meaning, but the exaggeration of tone directs the actor to make his speech heavily sarcastic—as, for example, in these lines:

> How it did grieve Macbeth! did he not straight
> In pious rage the two delinquents tear,
> That were the slaves of drink and thralls of sleep?

The unnamed Lord gives us information about Malcolm, and also makes the first reference in the play to the king of England, 'the most pious Edward', who is the complete opposite of Macbeth. The comparison will be developed in a later scene.

Act 4

Scene 1   We now see Macbeth receiving comfort from the three Apparitions that the witches call up. They appear in symbolic form. The first, 'an armed head', represents Macbeth's own head (wearing a helmet), as it is cut off and brought to Malcolm in *Act 5*, Scene 7. The 'bloody child' that comes next is Macduff, who had been 'untimely ripp'd' from his mother's womb (as he tells Macbeth in *Act 5*, Scene 7). And the last, the royal child with a tree in his hand, is Malcolm, the rightful king of Scotland, who approaches the palace at Dunsinane camouflaged with tree-branches (*Act 5*, Scene 4). Macbeth cannot interpret these symbols, but Shakespeare expects the audience to understand what is meant. This is 'dramatic irony'—when the truth of a situation is known to the audience but hidden from the characters in the play. There is dramatic irony, too, in the words spoken by the Apparitions, for again we understand the real meanings, while Macbeth can only understand the apparent meanings of the words. Macbeth, however, is in no doubt about the significance of the final 'show of Eight Kings'.

Scene 2   This pathetic scene in which Lady Macduff and her son are massacred shows us Macbeth's cruelty in action. When he plotted to kill Banquo's son, Fleance, he could justify the crime to himself by referring to the prophecy that Banquo's children should be kings. But he is in no danger from Lady Macduff or from her son; the crime is more dreadful because it is motiveless. Our knowledge of it helps us to find more dramatic irony in the scene that follows,

Scene 3   when Malcolm mistrusts Macduff chiefly because he cannot understand

> Why in that rawness left you wife and child—
> Those precious motives, those strong knots of love—
> Without leave-taking?

Macduff must prove his loyalty to Malcolm and to Scotland; then Malcolm must prove that he is worthy to be king. Again we are told of Edward the Confessor, and this time we hear of his divine gift of healing. This characteristic was not chosen by chance. Shakespeare uses many images of sickness; just a little later in this scene, he describes Scotland as a place where

> good men's lives
> Expire before the flowers in their caps,
> Dying or ere they sicken.

In Act 5 Scene 2 Caithness recognizes Malcolm as the doctor who can cure Scotland's sickness, calling him 'the medicine of the sickly weal' (line 27).

We respond intellectually to this account of the English king, and to the concept of the monarch as some kind of physician, divinely appointed to safeguard the country's health. We respond emotionally to the next episode in this long scene as Ross breaks the bad news to Macduff. We feel the painful irony of Ross's evasive answer: 'they were well at peace when I did leave 'em'. If we had not seen Lady Macduff and her son, we should not be distressed; because of scene 2, we are able to share Macduff's own grief. I am always moved by Macduff's answer to Malcolm, who urges him to

> Dispute it like a man.

Macduff replies with dignity

> I shall do so;
> But I must also feel it like a man.

The word 'man' is being used in two senses. Malcolm intends it to mean 'bravely', but Macduff is thinking of a man as a human being, with tender emotions of love and grief, which must not be denied.

Act 5

Scene 1   The very next scene shows what happens when human emotions are denied. At the beginning of the play Lady Macbeth prayed that she should know 'no compunctious visitings of nature' (1, 5, 44) that might prevent her from murdering Duncan. Now she walks in her sleep, and her mind constantly re-lives the night of the murder. On that night she declared confidently that 'A little water clears us of this deed' (2, 2, 67), but now she knows that 'all the perfumes of Arabia will not sweeten this little hand'. It is the last time we see Lady Macbeth. Although the Doctor warns her lady-in-waiting to 'Remove from her the means of all annoyance', we learn later that 'by self and violent hands', she killed herself (5, 7, 99).

Scene 2   From now until the end of the play the action moves between the two armies—Malcolm's soldiers, steadily drawing closer to Dunsinane, and Macbeth's forces, besieged near the castle. Caithness and Angus discuss the strength of the enemy, and Angus offers a shrewd comment on Macbeth:

> Now does he feel his title
> Hang loose about him, like a giant's robe
> Upon a dwarfish thief.

This is not the first image of badly-fitting clothes. When Macbeth was given the title 'thane of Cawdor', soon after the witches had prophesied that it would be given to him, he stood apart from Banquo and the king's messengers; then Banquo laughed, and explained that Macbeth was like a man with new clothes:

> New honours come upon him,
> Like our strange garments, cleave not to their mould
> But with the aid of use.   (*1*, 3, 144–6)

Macbeth himself thought of the praises he had earned for his courage in terms of fine clothes,

> Which would be worn now in their newest gloss,
> Not cast aside so soon.   (*1*, 7, 34–5)

There are many such allusions throughout the play. They make us stop and think about the relationship between Macbeth and the honours he is 'wearing'. Has he won them, or stolen them? Will his 'clothes' fit, in time—or will they always be too big for him?

Scene 3   When he has heard the Doctor's medical opinion of his wife, Macbeth asks, with his grim humour, for a medical opinion on the state of the country. The Doctor is allowed the same humour when he closes the scene:

> Were I from Dunsinane away and clear,
> Profit again should hardly draw me here.

The situation is now so serious that only a sour joke (playing on the Elizabethan belief in the doctor's greed for gold) can ease the tension.

Scene 4   Birnam Wood begins to move; what seemed like witches'
magic is seen to be elementary military tactics. Excitement and
tension mount, as the soldiers come closer to Dunsinane. But
Scene 5   Macbeth does not respond to the excitement: he has lost the
capacity for feeling either fear or, as we see when he hears of his
wife's death, grief. He speaks the most disillusioned words that
Shakespeare ever wrote when he contemplates life's 'petty pace
from day to day'. He still hopes that the witches' promises (made
to him in *Act 4*, Scene 1) will protect him; but when he hears that
'The wood began to move' his confidence is shaken, and he begins

> To doubt the equivocation of the fiend
> That lies like truth.

At this point we should remember the 'equivocator' that the Porter
joked about, long ago, in *Act 2*, Scene 3, and appreciate the way
that this whole play insists on the difference between *being* and
seeming, or between saying one thing and meaning another.
Scene 6   Continuous battle is now being waged, and the stage should
never be empty. Macbeth is at last forced to confront Macduff,
Scene 7   and also to confront the truth and admit that 'these juggling
fiends' cannot be trusted. When the castle has been surrendered,
Macbeth defeated, and victory proclaimed, Malcolm announces
the beginning of a new reign. Order has now been restored to
Scotland, and affairs will once again be conducted 'in measure,
time, and place'.

Macbeth: The man

Who can tell us more about a man's character than his wife? Shakespeare allows Lady Macbeth to explain her husband's character as she understands it, and although she cannot see the *whole* truth, she tells us a great deal about Macbeth that *is* true. Two lines of her soliloquy in *Act 1*, Scene 5 are particularly significant:

> Thou wouldst be great,
> Art not without ambition, but without
> The illness should attend it.   (*1*, 5, 17-19)

By 'illness' Lady Macbeth means 'evil', but her metaphor is appropriate: Macbeth 'catches' evil, as one might catch a disease. The play shows how his symptoms develop, until there is no hope of a cure, and the man must die.

We hear a lot about Macbeth before he comes on to the stage, first from the Sergeant who has fought on his side, and then from Ross, who also speaks of Macbeth's courage in battle. These reports lead us to expect a noble warrior and a loyal subject to Duncan. We have only one slight doubt about Macbeth, and we are not able to explain quite what this is. We know that, somehow, he is associated with the witches; and this, surely, cannot be good.

Macbeth speaks very little when first the witches, and then Ross, hail him as 'thane of Cawdor'. Perhaps he is stunned to silence by his good fortune. But soon we hear him speak—or rather, think aloud, for he does not mean to be overheard:

> Glamis, and thane of Cawdor;
> The greatest is behind.   (*1*, 3, 116-17)

Very soon he begins to admit a 'suggestion', some 'horrible imaginings', and then he says to himself the word 'murder' (*1*, 3, 134; 138; 139). Once this word has been spoken, we must regard Macbeth with suspicion, and the suspicion grows when he confesses his 'black and deep desires' in the scene that follows

(*1*, 4, 51). It is confirmed when his wife, speaking as though he were in the room with her, tells Macbeth that she knows he wants

> that which rather thou dost fear to do
> Than wishest should be undone.   (*1*, 5, 23-4)

It is not, however, cowardice that restrains Macbeth. At the end of *Act 1* he is wrestling with his conscience. He is acutely aware of the duty which he owes to Duncan:

> He's here in double trust:
> First, as I am his kinsman and his subject,
> Strong both against the deed; then as his host,
> Who should against his murderer shut the door,
> Not bear the knife myself.   (*1*, 7, 12-16)

These are profound reasons for curbing his ambition, but Macbeth continues the soliloquy. Even if he were not—as kinsman, subject, and host—in duty bound to defend Duncan, rather than harm him, there would still be enormous sin in killing the king. Macbeth appreciates Duncan's fine qualities—his humility and his integrity in carrying out to perfection the tasks of kingship; and he knows that to destroy such virtue would be a crime against heaven. He can appreciate Duncan's good qualities, and this is a virtue in Macbeth.

Before Lady Macbeth comes on to the scene, Macbeth has won a great victory over himself, and he is almost triumphant when he tells her, 'We will proceed no further in this business' (*1*, 7, 31).

But Lady Macbeth has no such conscience as her husband has. At this moment she is the stronger of the two, and Macbeth cannot stand up to her accusations that he is a coward, lacking in manliness, and a traitor to his word. He yields to her, and in order to prove himself a man in her eyes, submits to a woman's guidance.

After the murder of Duncan, Macbeth is horrified to think of what he has done. Again Shakespeare contrasts Macbeth and his wife in their attitudes to murder. Lady Macbeth is bold and confident, because she does not understand that the deed is morally wrong; her only concern is to destroy the evidence. Macbeth, however, awakens to a consciousness of guilt that will remain with him until his death.

Macbeth now has to act many parts. When the body of Duncan is discovered, he must appear as the loyal subject, appalled by the murder of his king. In speaking to the two Murderers whom he has hired to kill Banquo, he tries to show that he is a worthy ruler, distressed by injuries which have been inflicted on his subjects. And at the state banquet, probably his first public appearance since he was made king, he plays the part of host and friend to his thanes. He is not wholly successful in any of these rôles. When the murder is discovered, he over-acts to such an extent that his wife tries to draw attention from him by fainting. The Murderers are not interested in his efforts to justify the murder of Banquo: they have been hired to kill a man, and they will do the job they are paid to do. And the banquet is ruined for Macbeth by the appearance of Banquo's Ghost.

Macbeth appears again as himself (that is, not playing any 'part') at the end of *Act 3*, Scene 4, when he and his wife face each other across the remains of their banquet. He now knows that 'blood will have blood' (*1, 4, 122*), and that the first murder is *only* the first. A new character is emerging—a man who is so desperate that he must act and not stop to consider the reasons for acting:

> Strange things I have in head that will to hand,
> Which must be acted ere they may be scann'd.
>
> (*3, 4, 139–40*)

The last line here refers to an actor's part in a play, which ought to be 'scann'd'—that is, learned—before it is performed. With this comparison, Macbeth is beginning to recognize an unreality about his life.

The new Macbeth confronts the witches and demands to be answered; the answers give him a feeling of confidence which we, the audience, know to be unfounded. But Macbeth trusts no-one. He has no faith in the loyalty of the thanes, and sets spies on each one of them (see *3, 4, 131–2*); now it seems that he will not trust even the witches and their 'masters', for he is determined to 'make assurance double sure' (*4, 1, 83*) by slaughtering Macduff's entire family.

We do not see Macbeth for some time after his appearance in this scene with the witches. We hear a lot about him—and everything that we hear tells us that Macbeth has become a cruel tyrant, and that he has changed Scotland into a country 'Almost afraid to know itself' (*4, 3, 165*). There are more rumours to be heard when Malcolm's army moves towards Dunsinane; opinions about Macbeth vary:

> Some say he's mad; others, that lesser hate him,
> Do call it valiant fury.   (*5, 2, 13–14*)

He is indeed madly self-confident, believing that he is invincible:

> Till Birnam wood remove to Dunsinane
> I cannot taint with fear. What's the boy Malcolm?
> Was he not born of woman?   (5, 3, 2-4)

Alone, however, Macbeth is neither mad nor furious. He feels old and lonely:

> my way of life
> Is fall'n into the sere, the yellow leaf;
> And that which should accompany old age,
> As honour, love, obedience, troops of friends,
> I must not look to have.   (5, 3, 22-6)

Seyton tells him that his wife is dead, but he cannot grieve for her. Life has no meaning for him, and once again he sees himself as an actor,

> That struts and frets his hour upon the stage,
> And then is heard no more.   (5, 5, 25-6)

He has lost everything, and when he hears of the 'moving grove' (5, 5, 38) he knows that he is defeated.

Macbeth chooses to die in battle, 'with harness on our back' (5, 5, 52), and the decision perhaps revives a spark of our former respect for the mighty warrior. At last he is challenged by Macduff, and he is reluctant to fight:

> Of all men else I have avoided thee:
> But get thee back, my soul is too much charg'd
> With blood of thine already.   (5, 7, 33-5)

How should we interpret this? The first of the Apparitions told Macbeth to 'Beware Macduff'—is this why he has avoided him? Or is it guilt that has kept Macbeth from coming face-to-face with the man whose wife and children have been so brutally murdered? Is conscience returning with courage?

Characters in the play

Alex **Duncan** — *King of Scotland*

Mark Sayers **Malcolm** — *his sons*
Elizabeth **Donalbain**

Macbeth — *commanders of the Scottish army*
Mark Winborn **Banquo**

Keith **Macduff**
Wayne Mason **Lennox**
Jamie Southwest **Ross** — *thanes of Scotland*
Emma Davis **Menteith** (*thane*: a Scottish nobleman, just below
Emma Dangerfield **Angus** the rank of earl in the English nobility.)
Joanne Target **Caithness**

Sam **Fleance** — *Banquo's son*
Joanne Target **Boy** — *Macduff's son*
Elizabeth **Seyton** — *an officer attending Macbeth*
Steven Duckling **Siward** — *Earl of Northumberland, commander of the English army*
Raymond **Young Siward** — *his son*
Lady Macbeth
Kath Pass **Lady Macduff**

Emma — A Sergeant
A Porter
S. Duckling — An Old Man
Three Murderers
Brett — An English Doctor
A Scottish Doctor
1st *Jeanette* *Mandy* — A Gentlewoman attending Lady Macbeth
2nd *Julian* Three Witches
3rd *Martyn* Hecate *goddess and queen of witches*
The Ghost of Banquo
Apparitions
Lords, Attendants, Soldiers, Attendants, Messengers

Act I

Act I   scene I

A Prologue of evil. The witches plan
to meet Macbeth when the fighting has
finished.

moor : a wasteland area.

3   *hurlyburly :* fighting.

8   *Graymalkin :* grey cat.

9   *Paddock :* toad.

10 *Anon :* at once—I'm coming.

Scene I   *On the moor*

Thunder and lightning. Enter three Witches

First Witch
When shall we three meet again
In thunder, lightning, or in rain?

Second Witch
When the hurlyburly's done,
When the battle's lost and won.

Third Witch
5 That will be ere the set of sun.

First Witch
Where the place?

Second Witch   Upon the heath.

Third Witch
There to meet with Macbeth.

First Witch
I come, Graymalkin!

Second Witch
Paddock calls.

10 **Third Witch**   Anon.

All
Fair is foul, and foul is fair:
Hover through the fog and filthy air.   *[Exeunt*

Act I   scene 2

The good King Duncan hears news of
the battle. He is told how bravely
Macbeth and Banquo have fought
against the Norwegians and the
Scottish traitor, the Thane of Cawdor.
He declares that Macbeth shall be
rewarded with the title of 'Thane of
Cawdor'.

    Alarum: a battle call on a trumpet;
this shows that the scene is now a
military camp

2   *As . . . plight*: his wounded
condition suggests.

3   *newest state*: latest condition.

5   *'Gainst my captivity*: so that the
enemy did not capture me.

6   *broil*: conflict

8   *spent*: exhausted.

9   *choke their art*: hinder each other's
skill.

9-14   The rebel Scot, Macdonwald—who
is fit only to be a traitor because he has
so many vices—had the assistance ('is
supplied') of footsoldiers ('kerns') and
cavalry ('gallowglasses') from Ireland
and the Hebrides. Fortune, like a
prostitute, seemed to be also on his
side.

17   *steel*: sword.

18   *smok'd*: steamed.

19   *minion*: favourite.

21-2   Macbeth did not part from
Macdonwald until he had ripped him
open from the navel to the jaws.

25-8   But just as storms arise from the
east (where the sun rises), so from the
place where we expected hope, further
trouble arose.

Scene 2. *A camp near Forres*

    Alarum. Enter King Duncan, Malcolm,
    Donalbain, Lennox, *with* Attendants,
    meeting a bleeding Sergeant

Duncan
    What bloody man is that? He can report,
As seemeth by his plight, of the revolt
The newest state.
    Malcolm   This is the sergeant
Who, like a good and hardy soldier, fought
5 'Gainst my captivity. Hail, brave friend!
Say to the king the knowledge of the broil
As thou didst leave it.
    Sergeant   Doubtful it stood;
As two spent swimmers, that do cling together
And choke their art. The merciless Macdonwald—
10 Worthy to be a rebel, for to that
The multiplying villainies of nature
Do swarm upon him—from the western isles
Of kerns and gallowglasses is supplied;
And fortune, on his damned quarrel smiling,
15 Show'd like a rebel's whore: but all's too weak;
For brave Macbeth—well he deserves that
    name—
Disdaining fortune, with his brandish'd steel
Which smok'd with bloody execution,
Like valour's minion carv'd out his passage
20 Till he fac'd the slave;
Which ne'er shook hands, nor bade farewell to him,
Till he unseam'd him from the nave to the chaps,
And fix'd his head upon our battlements.
    Duncan
O valiant cousin! worthy gentleman!
    Sergeant
25 As whence the sun 'gins his reflection
Shipwracking storms and direful thunders break,
So from that spring, whence comfort seem'd to
    come,
Discomfort swells. Mark, King of Scotland, mark:
No sooner justice had, with valour arm'd,

30   Made these villains run away.

31-3   Sveno the Norwegian seized his chance, and with fresh arms and more men made a new attack.

36   *sooth*: truth.

37   *double cracks*: a double load of ammunition.

40-2   The sergeant cannot tell whether Macbeth and Banquo thought they would swim in blood, or make this scene of bloodshed as memorable ('memorize') as Golgotha (where Christ was crucified).

44-5   The soldier's words are as suitable for him as his wounds: both taste ('smack') of honour.

47   His eyes show he is in a hurry.

50   *flout*: scorn (the Norwegian flags have no right to be at Fife).

51-9   The king of Norway, with a fearful army and supported by the Thane of Cawdor, began to fight. Then Macbeth, who appeared like the husband of Bellona, goddess of war, clothed in strong armour ('lapp'd in proof'), opposed him with sword and courage like his own, until we won the battle.

---

30   Compell'd these skipping kerns to trust their heels,
But the Norweyan lord, surveying vantage,
With furbish'd arms and new supplies of men
Began a fresh assault.

Duncan   Dismay'd not this
Our captains, Macbeth and Banquo?

Sergeant   Yes;
35   As sparrows eagles, or the hare the lion.
If I say sooth, I must report they were
As cannons overcharg'd with double cracks;
So they
Doubly redoubled strokes upon the foe:
40   Except they meant to bathe in reeking wounds,
Or memorize another Golgotha,
I cannot tell—
But I am faint, my gashes cry for help.

Duncan
So well thy words become thee as thy wounds;
45   They smack of honour both. Go, get him surgeons.
[*Exit* Sergeant, *with other soldiers*

Enter Ross
Who comes here?

Malcolm   The worthy Thane of Ross.

Lennox
What a haste looks through his eyes! So should he look
That seems to speak things strange.

Ross   God save the king!

Duncan
Whence cam'st thou, worthy thane?

Ross   From Fife, great king;
50   Where the Norweyan banners flout the sky
And fan our people cold. Norway himself,
With terrible numbers,
Assisted by that most disloyal traitor,
The Thane of Cawdor, began a dismal conflict;
55   Till that Bellona's bridegroom, lapp'd in proof,
Confronted him with self-comparisons,

Point against point, rebellious arm 'gainst arm,
Curbing his lavish spirit: and, to conclude,
The victory fell on us.

Duncan   Great happiness!

Ross

60 That now
Sweno, the Norways' king, craves composition;
Nor would we deign him burial of his men
Till he disbursed, at Saint Colme's Inch,
Ten thousand dollars to our general use.

Duncan

65 No more that Thane of Cawdor shall deceive
Our bosom interest. Go pronounce his present
    death,
And with his former title greet Macbeth.

Ross

I'll see it done.

Duncan

What he hath lost noble Macbeth hath won.

[*Exeunt*

61   *craves composition :* begs for peace.

63   *disbursed :* paid.

66   *bosom interest :* love.
      present : immediate.

Act 1   scene 3

The witches assemble, and prepare to
meet Macbeth, who is travelling with
Banquo towards the king's camp at
Forres. The two men hear the witches'
prophecies with amazement, and then
Ross comes to them with a message
from Duncan.

Scene 3 *On the moor*

Thunder. Enter the three Witches

First Witch

Where hast thou been, sister?

Second Witch

Killing swine.

Third Witch

Sister, where thou?

First Witch

A sailor's wife had chestnuts in her lap,

5 And munch'd, and munch'd, and munch'd: 'Give
    me,' quoth I.
'Aroint thee, witch!' the rump-fed ronyon cries.
Her husband's to Aleppo gone, master o' the Tiger:
But in a sieve I'll thither sail,
And, like a rat without a tail,

10 I'll do, I'll do, and I'll do.

Second Witch

I'll give thee a wind,

6   *Aroint thee :* Go away!
     rump-fed ronyon : fat-bottomed old
woman.

First Witch
Th'art kind.
      Third Witch
And I another.
      First Witch
I myself have all the other;

14   *the other* : the other winds.

15 And the very ports they blow,
All the quarters that they know

17   *shipman's card* : compass.

I' the shipman's card.
I'll drain him dry as hay:
Sleep shall neither night nor day

20   *pent-house lid* : eyelid (which slopes like a shed leaning on the side of a house).
21   *forbid* : accursed.

20 Hang upon his pent-house lid;
He shall live a man forbid.
Weary sev'n-nights nine times nine
Shall he dwindle, peak and pine:
Though his bark cannot be lost,

24   *bark* : ship.

25 Yet it shall be tempest-tost.
Look what I have.
      Second Witch
Show me, show me.
      First Witch
Here I have a pilot's thumb,
Wreck'd as homeward he did come.
                    [A drum beats

      Third Witch
30 A drum! a drum!
Macbeth doth come.
      All
The weird sisters, hand in hand,

32   *weird* : supernatural.
33   *Posters* : fast travellers.

Posters of the sea and land,
Thus do go about, about:
35 Thrice to thine, and thrice to mine,
And thrice again, to make up nine.
Peace! the charm's wound up.

      Enter Macbeth *and* Banquo
      Macbeth
So foul and fair a day I have not seen.
      Banquo
How far is 't call'd to Forres? What are these,
40 So wither'd and so wild in their attire,
That look not like th' inhabitants o' the earth,
And yet are on 't? Live you? or are you aught
That man may question? You seem to under-
    stand me,

Macbeth
bunguo
meet witches
they tell the
future

44   *choppy* : chapped (rough and red).

By each at once her choppy finger laying
45 Upon her skinny lips: you should be women,
And yet your beards forbid me to interpret
That you are so.
   Macbeth Speak, if you can: what are you?
   First Witch
All hail, Macbeth! hail to thee, Thane of Glamis!
   Second Witch
All hail, Macbeth! hail to thee, Thane of Cawdor!
   Third Witch
50 All hail, Macbeth! that shalt be King hereafter.
   Banquo
Good sir, why do you start, and seem to fear

53-4   Are you imaginary, or as real as you
  seem to be?
54-7   You greet my friend with his
  present title, with prophecy of future
  nobility, and with promise of royalty,
  so that he seems amazed with it all.

Things that do sound so fair? I' the name of truth,
Are ye fantastical, or that indeed
Which outwardly ye show? My noble partner
55 You greet with present grace, and great prediction
Of noble having and of royal hope,
That he seems rapt withal: to me you speak not.
If you can look into the seeds of time,
And say which grain will grow and which will not,
60 Speak then to me, who neither beg nor fear,
Your favours nor your hate.
   First Witch
Hail!
   Second Witch
Hail!
   Third Witch
Hail!
   First Witch
65 Lesser than Macbeth, and greater.
   Second Witch
Not so happy, yet much happier.
   Third Witch

67   *get* : beget, be father of.

Thou shalt get kings, though thou be none:
So, all hail, Macbeth and Banquo!
   First Witch
Banquo and Macbeth, all hail!

You wont be king but you Child will be king

70   *imperfect* : unintelligible.

72   *the Thane of Cawdor lives*. Macbeth does not know of the Thane's treachery. Angus explains (lines 109–16) that he had conspired in secret with the king of Norway.

74   *Stands . . . belief* : is unbelievable.

81   *corporal* : solid, having a body.

82   *Would . . . stay'd!* I wish that they had stayed.

84   *the insane root* : hemlock, a drug that makes men mad.

91   *venture* : daring.

92–3   The king does not know whether to praise Macbeth or say how amazed he is.

96   *afeard* : afraid.

98   *post* : messenger.

98–9   The messengers all reported praise for what Macbeth had done in the defence of his country.

Macbeth

70 Stay, you imperfect speakers, tell me more:
    By Sinel's death I know I am Thane of Glamis;
    But how of Cawdor? the Thane of Cawdor lives,
    A prosperous gentleman; and to be king
    Stands not within the prospect of belief,
75 No more than to be Cawdor. Say from whence
    You owe this strange intelligence? or why
    Upon this blasted heath you stop our way
    With such prophetic greeting? Speak, I charge you.
                                    [Witches *vanish*

Banquo

    The earth hath bubbles, as the water has,
80 And these are of them. Whither are they vanish'd?

Macbeth

    Into the air, and what seem'd corporal melted,
    As breath into the wind. Would they had stay'd!

Banquo

    Were such things here as we do speak about?
    Or have we eaten on the insane root
85 That takes the reason prisoner?

Macbeth

    Your children shall be kings.

Banquo   You shall be king.

Macbeth

    And Thane of Cawdor too; went it not so?

Banquo

    To the self-same tune and words. Who's here?

                    Enter Ross *and* Angus

Ross

    The king hath happily receiv'd, Macbeth,
90 The news of thy success; and when he reads
    Thy personal venture in the rebels' fight,
    His wonders and his praises do contend
    Which should be thine or his. Silenc'd with that,
    In viewing o'er the rest o' the self-same day,
95 He finds thee in the stout Norweyan ranks,
    Nothing afeard of what thyself didst make,
    Strange images of death. As thick as hail
    Came post with post, and every one did bear

Thy praises in his kingdom's great defence,
100 And pour'd them down before him.
    Angus   We are sent
To give thee from our royal master thanks;
Only to herald thee into his sight,
Not pay thee.
    Ross
And, for an earnest of a greater honour,
105 He bade me, from him, call thee Thane of Cawdor:
In which addition, hail, most worthy Thane!
For it is thine.
    Banquo [*Aside*] What! can the devil speak true
    Macbeth
The Thane of Cawdor lives: why do you dress me
In borrow'd robes?
    Angus   Who was the Thane lives yet;
110 But under heavy judgment bears that life
Which he deserves to lose. Whether he was combin'd
With those of Norway, or did line the rebel
With hidden help or vantage, or that with both
He labour'd in his country's wreck, I know not;
115 But treasons capital, confess'd and prov'd,
Have overthrown him.
    Macbeth
           [*Aside*] Glamis, and Thane of Cawdor:
The greatest is behind. [*To* Ross *and* Angus]
                      Thanks for your pains.
[*To* Banquo] Do you not hope your children shall be kings,
When those that gave the Thane of Cawdor to me
120 Promis'd no less to them?
    Banquo   That, trusted home,
Might yet enkindle you unto the crown,
Besides the Thane of Cawdor. But 'tis strange:
And oftentimes, to win us to our harm,
The instruments of darkness tell us truths,
125 Win us with honest trifles, to betray's
In deepest consequence.
Cousins, a word, I pray you.

101   Ross and Angus bring thanks from Duncan to greet Macbeth as he comes before the king, but these thanks are not the only payment he will receive.

104   *earnest*: a token, promising more reward.

106   *addition*: additional title.

111   *combin'd*: allied.

112   *line*: strengthen (as the lining strengthens a garment).

113   *vantage*: advantage (perhaps the traitor gave the foreign enemies a base in Scotland from which they could attack).

115   *treasons capital*: treasons which are punishable by death.

117   *the greatest is behind*: the greatest of the three prophecies is the last of them, and has not happened yet.
    pains: trouble.

120   *trusted home*: trusted completely.
121   *enkindle*: set your hopes on fire.

123-6   Often, to bring about our damnation, the agents of evil tell us simple truths, so that we trust them; then they deceive us in important matters.

127   *Cousins*: Friends.

128-9	Macbeth sees his future before him as though it were a mighty play on the theme of kingship.

Macbeth   [*Aside*]   Two truths are told,
As happy prologues to the swelling act
Of the imperial theme. [*Aloud*] I thank you,
   gentlemen.

130	*soliciting* : persuasion.

130 [*Aside*] This supernatural soliciting
Cannot be ill, cannot be good; if ill,
Why hath it given me earnest of success,
Commencing in a truth? I am Thane of Cawdor:
If good, why do I yield to that suggestion

136	*seated* : firmly fixed.

135 Whose horrid image doth unfix my hair
And make my seated heart knock at my ribs,
Against the use of nature? Present fears
Are less than horrible imaginings;

139-42	Macbeth's mind, which thinks of murder as merely fantastical, disturbs his whole being. He can do nothing because he is wondering what will happen ('surmise'). Only the future ('what is not') is real to him.

My thought, whose murder yet is but fantastical,
140 Shakes so my single state of man that function
Is smother'd in surmise, and nothing is
But what is not.

142	*rapt* : amazed, lost in his own thoughts.

Banquo   Look, how our partner's rapt.
Macbeth
[*Aside*] If chance will have me king, why, chance
   may crown me,

144	*Without my stir* : Without any effort from me.

Without my stir.
Banquo   New honours come upon him,

145-6	New clothes do not fit ('cleave to') our bodies until we are accustomed to them.

145 Like our strange garments, cleave not to their
   mould

146-7	Let what is going to happen, happen; even the hardest day comes to an end.

But with the aid of use.
Macbeth   [*Aside*]   Come what come may,
Time and the hour runs through the roughest day.
Banquo

148	*stay* : wait.

Worthy Macbeth, we stay upon your leisure.
Macbeth
Give me your favour: my dull brain was wrought

150-2	His memory is like a book, which he reads every day, and he will always remember their efforts ('pains').

150 With things forgotten. Kind gentlemen, your pains
Are register'd where every day I turn
The leaf to read them. Let us toward the King.
[*To* Banquo] Think upon what hath chanc'd; and,
   at more time,

154	*interim* : meanwhile. Between the present, and a future meeting with Banquo, Macbeth will have had time to think about what has happened ('chanc'd').
155	*free* : honest.

The interim having weigh'd it, let us speak
155 Our free hearts each to other.
Banquo   Very gladly.

Macbeths career.
Start good soldier. very brave
very loyal. but witches put bad idea in
head, he got bad his is aly led.

Macbeth

Till then, enough. Come, friends.   [*Exeunt*

Act 1   scene 4

Duncan receives Macbeth and Banquo,
and tells the company that his son
Malcolm is next heir to the throne of
Scotland.

Flourish : Fanfare, heralding the
royal procession.

2   *in commission* : in charge of the
       execution.
       liege : lord.

6   *set forth* : showed.

9   *studied in* : practised.
10   *ow'd* : owned.
11-12 One cannot learn to know a man's
       mind by looking at his face.

16-20 Macbeth, in his deserving, is far
       ahead of any payment. Duncan wishes
       he had deserved less, so that his thanks
       and reward might be more in
       proportion.

21   *thy due* : due to you.

23   *pays itself* : is its own reward.

26-7   It is no more than our duty to do
       everything we can to ensure the safety
       of your love and honour.

Scene 4 *Forres. A room in the palace*

Flourish. Enter Duncan, Malcolm,
      Donalbain, Lennox, *and* Attendants

Duncan

Is execution done on Cawdor? Are not
Those in commission yet return'd?

Malcolm   My liege,

They are not yet come back; but I have spoke
With one that saw him die; who did report
5   That very frankly he confess'd his treasons,
Implor'd your highness' pardon, and set forth
A deep repentance. Nothing in his life
Became him like the leaving it; he died
As one that had been studied in his death,
10   To throw away the dearest thing he ow'd,
As 'twere a careless trifle.

Duncan   There's no art
To find the mind's construction in the face:
He was a gentleman on whom I built
An absolute trust.

Enter Macbeth, Banquo, Ross, *and* Angus
                            O worthiest cousin!
15   The sin of my ingratitude even now
Was heavy on me. Thou art so far before,
That swiftest wing of recompense is slow
To overtake thee; would thou hadst less deserv'd,
That the proportion both of thanks and payment
20   Might have been mine! Only I have left to say,
More is thy due than more than all can pay.

Macbeth

The service and the loyalty I owe,
In doing it, pays itself. Your highness' part
Is to receive our duties; and our duties
25   Are to your throne and state, children and servants;
Which do but what they should, by doing every-
      thing
Safe toward your love and honour.

Duncan   Welcome hither:
I have begun to plant thee, and will labour
To make thee full of growing. Noble Banquo,
30 That hast no less deserv'd, nor must be known
No less to have done so, let me infold thee
And hold thee to my heart.
Banquo   There if I grow,
The harvest is your own.
Duncan   My plenteous joys
Wanton in fulness, seek to hide themselves
35 In drops of sorrow. Sons, kinsmen, thanes,
And you whose places are the nearest, know
We will establish our estate upon
Our eldest, Malcolm, whom we name hereafter
The Prince of Cumberland; which honour must
40 Not unaccompanied invest him only,
But signs of nobleness, like stars, shall shine
On all deservers. [*To* Macbeth] From hence to
    Inverness,
And bind us further to you.
Macbeth
The rest is labour, which is not us'd for you:
45 I'll be myself the harbinger, and make joyful
The hearing of my wife with your approach;
So, humbly take my leave.
Duncan   My worthy Cawdor!
Macbeth
[*Aside*] The Prince of Cumberland! that is a step
On which I must fall down, or else o'er-leap,
50 For in my way it lies. Stars, hide your fires!
Let not light see my black and deep desires;
The eye wink at the hand; yet let that be
Which the eye fears, when it is done, to see. [*Exit*
Duncan
True, worthy Banquo; he is full so valiant,
55 And in his commendations I am fed;
It is a banquet to me. Let's after him,
Whose care is gone before to bid us welcome:
It is a peerless kinsman.   [*Flourish. Exeunt*

34   *Wanton :* Unrestrained.

36   *the nearest :* nearest to the throne, in line of succession.

37-42 Duncan names Malcolm as his successor, giving him the title 'Prince of Cumberland' (just as the Prince of Wales is heir to the English throne). Malcolm will not be the only one to be honoured; titles will be bestowed on all who deserve them.

42   *Inverness :* i.e. Macbeth's castle.

43   *bind us further :* increase our debt.

44   Resting-time is more like hard work, when it is not used for the king.

45   *harbinger :* herald.

52   *The eye wink at the hand :* let the eye not see what the hand is doing.

58   *peerless :* without an equal.

Act 1   scene 5
Lady Macbeth reads her husband's
letter; then she and Macbeth talk of
their plans.

5   *rapt* : amazed.

8   *coming on of time* : future.

10   *deliver thee* : report to you.
11   *dues of rejoicing* : your share of the
rejoicing.

Scene 5 *Inverness. A room in Macbeth's castle*

Enter Lady Macbeth, *reading a letter*
Lady Macbeth
*'They met me in the day of success; and I have learned
by the perfectest report, they have more in them than
mortal knowledge. When I burned in desire to question
them further, they made themselves air, into which they*
5 *vanished. Whiles I stood rapt in the wonder of it, came
missives from the king, who all-hailed me, "Thane of
Cawdor"; by which title, before, these weird sisters
saluted me, and referred me to the coming on of time,
with, "Hail, king that shalt be!" This have I thought*
10 *good to deliver thee, my dearest partner of greatness,
that thou mightest not lose the dues of rejoicing, by
being ignorant of what greatness is promised thee. Lay
it to thy heart, and farewell.'*

Glamis thou art, and Cawdor; and shalt be
15 What thou art promis'd. Yet do I fear thy nature;
It is too full o' the milk of human kindness
To catch the nearest way. Thou wouldst be great,
Art not without ambition, but without

19   *illness . . . it :* evil that must accompany ambition.

The illness should attend it; what thou wouldst highly,
20 That wouldst thou holily; wouldst not play false,
And yet wouldst wrongly win; thou'dst have, great Glamis,

22   *That :* i.e. the crown.

That which cries, 'Thus thou must do', if thou have it;
And that which rather thou dost fear to do
Than wishest should be undone. Hie thee hither,
25 That I may pour my spirits in thine ear,

26   *chastise :* drive away.
27   *golden round :* crown.
28   *metaphysical :* supernatural (i.e. helped by the witches).

And chastise with the valour of my tongue
All that impedes thee from the golden round,
Which fate and metaphysical aid doth seem
To have thee crown'd withal.

Enter a Messenger

29   *tidings :* news.

What is your tidings?
Messenger
30 The king comes here to-night.
Lady Macbeth   Thou 'rt mad to say it.
Is not thy master with him? who, were't so,
Would have inform'd for preparation.

31-2 Macbeth would have told her that the king was coming, so that she could make preparations.

Messenger
So please you, it is true: our thane is coming;
One of my fellows had the speed of him,

34   *had the speed of him :* travelled faster than he did.

35 Who, almost dead for breath, had scarcely more
Than would make up his message.

36   *tending :* care, attention.

Lady Macbeth   Give him tending;
He brings great news. [*Exit* Messenger] The raven himself is hoarse

40   *tend :* attend, wait.
unsex me : take away all that makes me a woman (such as tenderness, love, and pity).

That croaks the fatal entrance of Duncan
Under my battlements. Come, you spirits

42   *direst :* worst.
42-6 *make . . . and it :* make me insensitive, by blocking up all the pathways by which remorse can reach my heart, so that no natural feelings of conscience make me hesitate in my wicked ('fell') plans, or come between my scheme and the carrying-out ('th' effect') of this scheme.

40 That tend on mortal thoughts! unsex me here,
And fill me from the crown to the toe top-full
Of direst cruelty; make thick my blood,
Stop up the access and passage to remorse,
That no compunctious visitings of nature

45   Shake my fell purpose, nor keep peace between
     Th' effect and it! Come to my woman's breasts,
     And take my milk for gall, you murdering ministers,
     Wherever in your sightless substances
     You wait on nature's mischief! Come, thick night,
50   And pall thee in the dunnest smoke of hell,
     That my keen knife see not the wound it makes,
     Nor heaven peep through the blanket of the dark,
     To cry, 'Hold, hold!'

       Enter Macbeth
                Great Glamis! worthy Cawdor!
     Greater than both, by the all-hail hereafter!
55   Thy letters have transported me beyond
     This ignorant present, and I feel now
     The future in the instant.
       Macbeth   My dearest love,
     Duncan comes here to-night.
       Lady Macbeth   And when goes hence?
       Macbeth
     To-morrow, as he purposes.
       Lady Macbeth   O never
60   Shall sun that morrow see!
     Your face, my thane, is as a book where men
     May read strange matters. To beguile the time,
     Look like the time; bear welcome in your eye,
     Your hand, your tongue: look like the innocent
       flower
65   But be the serpent under 't. He that's coming
     Must be provided for; and you shall put
     This night's great business into my dispatch;
     Which shall to all our nights and days to come
     Give solely sovereign sway and masterdom.
       Macbeth
70   We will speak further.
       Lady Macbeth   Only look up clear;
     To alter favour ever is to fear.
     Leave all the rest to me.   *[Exeunt*

47 *gall :* a bitter liquid, secreted in the liver.

48 *sightless :* invisible. Although the 'spirits' that Lady Macbeth invokes are real—they have 'substances'—they cannot be seen.

50 *pall :* shroud.
    dunnest : darkest.

54 *all-hail hereafter :* future prophecy.

57 *The future in the instant.* She is transported, in her imagination, into the future, and feels that this is already present ('in the instant').

62 *beguile :* deceive.

63 *Look like the time :* put on the appropriate appearance (which now is that of the welcoming host).

67 *dispatch :* management.

69 *solely sovereign sway :* nothing less than the power of a king.

70 *clear :* with an honest face.

71 Fear always shows itself in a change of expression.

Act I   scene 6

Duncan and his court arrive at Macbeth's castle, and are welcomed by Lady Macbeth.

1   *seat* : situation.

2   *Nimbly* : freshly.

4   *martlet* : house-martin, a bird that often nests in churches.

       approve : prove.

5   *mansionry* : building.

6–8 The birds' nests hang (are 'pendent') on every convenient ('of vantage') jutting-out piece of the architecture of the castle, and these nests are the cradles for the young birds.

11–14 'I am sometimes embarrassed by the love that is shown to me ("follows us"), but I am always ("still") grateful, because it *is* love. In this I am teaching you to ask God to reward ("'eyld" = yield) me for the trouble ("pains") that *you* are having to take, and also to thank *me* for that trouble.' In this polite joke with Lady Macbeth, Duncan suggests that she will be a better person for this trouble, and therefore she should thank him for giving her the chance to improve.

15   If every part were done twice, and then twice again.

18   *those of old* : those honours bestowed in the past.

19   *late* : recent.

20   *hermits.* Lady Macbeth and her husband will be like holy men who offer prayers for their benefactors.

21   *cours'd* : chased.

       at the heels : closely.

Scene 6 *Outside Macbeth's castle*

Music and torches. Enter Duncan, Malcolm, Donalbain, Banquo, Lennox, Macduff, Ross, Angus, *and* Attendants

Duncan

This castle hath a pleasant seat; the air
Nimbly and sweetly recommends itself
Unto our gentle senses.

Banquo   This guest of summer,
The temple-haunting martlet, does approve,
5 By his lov'd mansionry, that the heaven's breath
Smells wooingly here: no jutty, frieze,
Buttress, nor coign of vantage, but this bird
Hath made his pendent bed and procreant cradle:
Where they most breed and haunt, I have observ'd
10 The air is delicate.

Enter Lady Macbeth

Duncan   See, see, our honour'd hostess!
The love that follows us sometime is our trouble,
Which still we thank as love. Herein I teach you
How you shall bid God 'eyld us for your pains,
And thank us for your trouble.

Lady Macbeth   All our service,
15 In every point twice done, and then done double,
Were poor and single business, to contend
Against those honours deep and broad, wherewith
Your majesty loads our house: for those of old,
And the late dignities heap'd up to them,
20 We rest your hermits.

Duncan   Where's the Thane of Cawdor?
We cours'd him at the heels, and had a purpose
To be his purveyor; but he rides well,
And his great love, sharp as his spur, hath holp him
To his home before us. Fair and noble hostess,
25 We are your guest to-night.

Lady Macbeth   Your servants ever
Have theirs, themselves, and what is theirs, in compt,
To make their audit at your highness' pleasure,
Still to return your own.

22   *purveyor :* the official who went before a king to arrange for his reception.

23   *holp :* helped.

25-8   The king's servants hold everything in trust ('in compt') for the king, and they will give an account ('make . . . audit') whenever the king asks for one, and always ('still') return everything back to him.

31   *By your leave.* A courteous remark: Duncan may perhaps kiss Lady Macbeth's hand, or take her arm, and go into the castle with her.

Act 1   scene 7

Macbeth prepares for murder. He knows that this is a great sin, but his wife forces him to do the deed.

1-2   *If . . . quickly :* if the business of the murder were ended ('done') as soon as the murder is performed ('done'), then it would be a good thing to have it carried out ('done') quickly.

2-4   *if . . . success :* if the assassination could prevent ('trammel' = entangle, enmesh) any further consequences, and succeed as soon as it ended ('With his surcease').

4   *his :* its.
      but this blow : this single blow.

5   *the be-all and the end-all :* all that is needed to end everything.

6   *upon this bank and shoal of time :* in this life. Macbeth imagines Time as a sandbank or shallow place ('shoal') in the sea of eternity.

7   *We'd jump the life to come :* I would take no notice of an eternal life after death (where there might be punishment for earthly sins).

7-8   *But . . . here :* for crimes like this, there is still judgement on earth.

8-10   *that . . . inventor :* we only teach others lessons in murder, and after the lessons have been learned, they come back to torment the man who first found them out.

10   *even-handed :* fair-minded.

11   *Commends :* prescribes.
      chalice : cup, especially one used in religious ceremonies.

Duncan   Give me your hand;
Conduct me to mine host: we love him highly,
30 And shall continue our graces towards him.
By your leave, hostess.   [*Exeunt*

Scene 7 *A room in Macbeth's castle*

Music and torches. Servants, carrying dishes for a feast, hurry across the stage. Then enter Macbeth

Macbeth
If it were done, when 'tis done, then 'twere well
It were done quickly; if th' assassination
Could trammel up the consequence, and catch,
With his surcease, success; that but this blow
5 Might be the be-all and the end-all—here,
But here, upon this bank and shoal of time,
We'd jump the life to come. But in these cases,
We still have judgement here; that we but teach
Bloody instructions, which, being taught, return
10 To plague the inventor; this even-handed justice
Commends the ingredients of our poison'd chalice
To our own lips. He's here in double trust:
First, as I am his kinsman and his subject,
Strong both against the deed; then, as his host,
15 Who should against his murderer shut the door,
Not bear the knife myself. Besides, this Duncan
Hath borne his faculties so meek, hath been
So clear in his great office, that his virtues
Will plead like angels, trumpet-tongu'd, against
20 The deep damnation of his taking-off;
And pity, like a naked new-born babe,
Striding the blast, or heaven's cherubin, hors'd
Upon the sightless couriers of the air,
Shall blow the horrid deed in every eye,
25 That tears shall drown the wind. I have no spur
To prick the sides of my intent, but only
Vaulting ambition, which o'er-leaps itself
And falls on the other.

Enter Lady Macbeth
                        How now! what news?

14 *Strong . . . deed.* Macbeth is both Duncan's kinsman and Duncan's subject, and these are two strong reasons to prevent this murder.

16-25 Duncan has been so fine a king that if he is murdered his virtues will have the powers of angels, and voices like trumpets, to cry out against the deed. Pity itself will be seen, as tender as a baby; and the cherubin (the highest order of angels) will ride on the winds and blow news of the crime into every man's eye, until so many tears will be shed that the winds themselves are drowned.

17 *borne . . . meek :* has been so humble in exercising the powers ('faculties') of a king.

18 *clear :* honourable.

20 *taking-off :* murder.

23 *sightless couriers :* invisible messengers (the winds).

25-8 Ambition is Macbeth's only motive, and his ambition is like a horse that tries to jump too high ('o'er-leaps itself') and falls on the other side of the fence.

32-5 Macbeth wants to enjoy the praises he has earned ('bought') as though they were new clothes. If he proceeds with the murder of Duncan he will lose men's good opinions of him, and it will be like throwing away his new clothes.

37 *green and pale :* sickly (as if the hope had a hangover).

39 *afeard :* afraid. Are you frightened to be in fact what you would like to be?

44 *wait upon :* follow.

45 *adage :* proverb. The saying is 'The cat would eat fish, but would not wet her feet'.
 Prithee : I pray thee.

46 *become :* be fitting for.

47 He who dares do more than is fitting for a man, is no man at all (he becomes a beast).

48 *break :* mention.

49 *durst :* dare (past tense).

Lady Macbeth

He has almost supp'd: why have you left the chamber?

Macbeth

30 Hath he ask'd for me?

Lady Macbeth   Know you not, he has?

Macbeth

We will proceed no further in this business:
He hath honour'd me of late; and I have bought
Golden opinions from all sorts of people,
Which would be worn now in their newest gloss,
35 Not cast aside so soon.

Lady Macbeth   Was the hope drunk,
Wherein you dress'd yourself? hath it slept since,
And wakes it now, to look so green and pale
At what it did so freely? From this time
Such I account thy love. Art thou afeard
40 To be the same in thine own act and valour
As thou art in desire? Wouldst thou have that
Which thou esteem'st the ornament of life,
And live a coward in thine own esteem,
Letting 'I dare not' wait upon 'I would',
45 Like the poor cat i' the adage?

Macbeth   Prithee, peace.
I dare do all that may become a man;
Who dares do more, is none.

Lady Macbeth   What beast was't, then,
That made you break this enterprise to me?
When you durst do it, then you were a man;
50 And, to be more than what you were, you would
Be so much more the man. Nor time nor place
Did then adhere, and yet you would make both:
They have made themselves, and that their fitness now
Does unmake you. I have given suck, and know
55 How tender 'tis to love the babe that milks me:
I would, while it was smiling in my face,
Have pluck'd my nipple from his boneless gums,
And dash'd the brains out, had I so sworn as you
Have done to this.

Macbeth   If we should fail—

Lady Macbeth   We fail?

51-4 When Macbeth first suggested the murder, neither time nor place was suitable, yet he would find a time and a place. Now both time and place are right, but because they are right he is afraid—made no longer a man.

60   *sticking-place.* The strings of a lute, or a modern guitar, are tightened and tuned by screwing the pegs to which they are fastened. Macbeth must screw up his courage like a guitar-string, until it is taut and has reached its 'sticking-place'.

64-7 I will overpower ('convince') his two attendants with wine and merry-making ('wassail') so that their memory, which guards the brain (according to Elizabethan anatomy) shall be a fog ('fume'), and the brain itself, the place where reason is received ('receipt of reason'), shall be no more than a chemist's distilling-flask ('limbeck').

68   *drenched:* soaked, drunken.

71   *spongy*—because they have soaked up so much wine, like sponges.

72   *quell:* kill, murder.

73   *mettle:* courage.

74   *receiv'd:* accepted.

77-8 Who will dare believe anything else, since we shall cry out with so much grief and noise?

79   *bend up:* make ready.

80   *corporal agent:* physical faculty.

81   *mock:* deceive.

60 But screw your courage to the sticking-place,
And we'll not fail. When Duncan is asleep,
Whereto the rather shall his day's hard journey
Soundly invite him, his two chamberlains
Will I with wine and wassail so convince,
65 That memory, the warder of the brain,
Shall be a fume, and the receipt of reason
A limbeck only; when in swinish sleep
Their drenched natures lie, as in a death,
What cannot you and I perform upon
70 The unguarded Duncan? what not put upon
His spongy officers, who shall bear the guilt
Of our great quell?

    Macbeth   Bring forth men-children only!
For thy undaunted mettle should compose
Nothing but males. Will it not be receiv'd,
75 When we have mark'd with blood those sleepy two
Of his own chamber, and us'd their very daggers,
That they have done 't?

    Lady Macbeth   Who dares receive it other,
As we shall make our griefs and clamour roar
Upon his death?

    Macbeth   I am settled, and bend up
80 Each corporal agent to this terrible feat.
Away, and mock the time with fairest show:
False face must hide what the false heart doth
    know.   *[Exeunt*

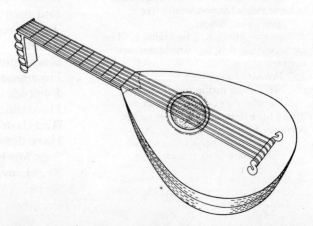

Act 2

Banquo and his son Fleance are on
their way to bed when they meet
Macbeth. He is nervously waiting the
signal to murder Duncan.

1   What time is it?

2   *is down :* has set.

3   *she :* the moon.

4   *husbandry :* economy

5   *Their candles :* the stars.
         that. Banquo perhaps gives his
cloak to Fleance.
6-9   Banquo feels heavy with sleep, as
though he is called to bed, yet he wants
to keep awake. He is afraid of the
thoughts that come when the body is
at rest.

14   *largess :* gifts.
         offices : servants' quarters.
15-16   *greets . . . hostess :* he addresses it
to your wife, as his most kind hostess.
16   *shut up :* ended the day.

Scene 1 *The courtyard of Macbeth's castle*

Enter Banquo *and* Fleance, *with a*
Servant *bearing a torch before them*

Banquo
How goes the night, boy?
Fleance
The moon is down; I have not heard the clock.
Banquo
And she goes down at twelve.
Fleance   I take 't, 'tis later, sir.
Banquo
Hold, take my sword. There's husbandry in
    heaven;
5 Their candles are all out. Take thee that too.
A heavy summons lies like lead upon me,
And yet I would not sleep: merciful powers,
Restrain in me the cursed thoughts that nature
Gives way to in repose.

Enter Macbeth, *and a* Servant *with a torch*
                            Give me my sword.
10 Who's there?
Macbeth
A friend.
Banquo
What, sir! not yet at rest? The king's a-bed:
He hath been in unusual pleasure, and
Sent forth great largess to your offices.
15 This diamond he greets your wife withal,
By the name of most kind hostess; and shut up
In measureless content.

17-19 We were not prepared, and so we
could not be as generous ('free') as we
wished.

22   *an hour to serve :* a convenient
time.

24   *At your kind'st leisure :* whenever
you would be so kind as to spare the
time.
25   If you will follow my advice, when
the time comes.
26   *So :* provided that.
27   *augment :* increase.
28   *bosom franchis'd :* heart free from
guilt.
        clear : loyal (to the king).
29   *be counsell'd :* listen to your advice.

36-7   *sensible . . . sight :* able to be felt as
well as seen.

39   *heat-oppressed :* feverish.
40   *palpable :* touchable.

42   *marshall'st :* beckons.

Macbeth   Being unprepar'd,
Our will became the servant to defect,
Which else should free have wrought.
Banquo   All's well.
20 I dreamt last night of the three weird sisters:
To you they have show'd some truth.
Macbeth   I think not of them:
Yet, when we can entreat an hour to serve,
We would spend it in some words upon that
    business,
If you would grant the time.
Banquo   At your kind'st leisure.
Macbeth
25 If you shall cleave to my consent, when 'tis,
It shall make honour for you.
Banquo   So I lose none
In seeking to augment it, but still keep
My bosom franchis'd and allegiance clear,
I shall be counsell'd.
Macbeth   Good repose the while!
Banquo
30 Thanks, sir: the like to you.
                    [*Exeunt* Banquo *and* Fleance
Macbeth
Go bid thy mistress, when my drink is ready,
She strike upon the bell. Get thee to bed.
                              [*Exit* Servant
Is this a dagger which I see before me,
The handle toward my hand? Come, let me clutch
    thee:
35 I have thee not, and yet I see thee still.
Art thou not, fatal vision, sensible
To feeling as to sight? or art thou but
A dagger of the mind, a false creation,
Proceeding from the heat-oppressed brain?
40 I see thee yet, in form as palpable
As this which now I draw.
Thou marshall'st me the way that I was going;

44–5	Either his eyes are foolish, compared to the other senses, or they are more trustworthy than all the rest.
46	*dudgeon*: hilt. *gouts*: drops.
48–9	*informs Thus*: takes shape in this way.
49	*one half-world*: the hemisphere that is in darkness.
50	*abuse*: deceive.
51	*curtain'd*. The curtains are those of the four-poster bed, rather than window-curtains. *celebrates*: performs the rites ('offerings').
52	*Hecate*: goddess of witches.
53	*Alarum'd*: woken up (as by a modern alarm-clock). *sentinel*: guard, watchman.
54	*Whose howl's his watch*: the wolf's howl is like the cry of the night-watchman (who patrolled the streets of Elizabethan London).
55	*Tarquin*. Murder has been personified in line 52, and is now compared to the Roman Tarquin, who came in the night to rape ('ravish') his friend's wife, Lucrece. Shakespeare wrote a long poem, *The Rape of Lucrece*, on this subject. *design*: aim.
58	*prate*: chatter.
59–60	*take . . . with it*: break the present horrible silence which is appropriate at this time.
60	*threat*: threaten.
61	Words are only breath, which is cold; deeds must be hot.
63	*knell*: funeral bell.

And such an instrument I was to use.
Mine eyes are made the fools o' the other senses,
45 Or else worth all the rest: I see thee still;
And on thy blade and dudgeon gouts of blood,
Which was not so before. There's no such thing:
It is the bloody business which informs
Thus to mine eyes. Now o'er the one half-world
50 Nature seems dead, and wicked dreams abuse
The curtain'd sleep; witchcraft celebrates
Pale Hecate's offerings; and wither'd murder,
Alarum'd by his sentinel, the wolf,
Whose howl's his watch, thus with his stealthy pace,
55 With Tarquin's ravishing strides, toward his design
Moves like a ghost. Thou sure and firm-set earth,
Hear not my steps, which way they walk, for fear
Thy very stones prate of my whereabout,
And take the present horror from the time,
60 Which now suits with it. Whiles I threat, he lives:
Words to the heat of deeds too cold breath gives.
                                        [*A bell rings*

I go, and it is done; the bell invites me.
Hear it not, Duncan; for it is a knell
That summons thee to heaven, or to hell.   [*Exit*

Act 2   scene 2

Lady Macbeth waits for her husband, who comes from Duncan's room with bloody hands.

1   *them* : Duncan's attendants.

2   *quench'd* : cooled, put out the fire.

4   *owl* : a bird of the night; the owl is compared to the man who rang the funeral ('fatal') bell outside the cells of prisoners condemned to die in Newgate prison.

5   *about it* : doing the deed.
6   *surfeited grooms* : drunken servants.
7   *possets* : hot drinks, 'nightcaps'.

8–9   Death and Life fight over the attendants to decide whether they should live or die.

12   *Confounds* : ruins.

16   *crickets* : chirping insects (which were thought by the Elizabethans to herald death).

21   *sorry* : miserable.

Scene 2 *The courtyard of Macbeth's castle*

Enter Lady Macbeth

Lady Macbeth
That which hath made them drunk hath made me bold,
What hath quench'd them hath given me fire. Hark! Peace!
It was the owl that shriek'd, the fatal bellman,
5 Which gives the stern'st good-night. He is about it:
The doors are open, and the surfeited grooms
Do mock their charge with snores: I have drugg'd their possets,
That death and nature do contend about them,
Whether they live or die.

Macbeth
[*Within*]   Who's there? what, ho!

Lady Macbeth
10 Alack! I am afraid they have awak'd,
And 'tis not done; the attempt and not the deed
Confounds us. Hark! I laid their daggers ready;
He could not miss 'em. Had he not resembled
My father as he slept, I had done't.

Enter Macbeth

My husband!

Macbeth
15 I have done the deed. Didst thou not hear a noise?

Lady Macbeth
I heard the owl scream and the crickets cry.
Did not you speak?

Macbeth   When?

Lady Macbeth   Now.

Macbeth   As I descended?

Lady Macbeth
Ay.

Macbeth
Hark!
20 Who lies i' the second chamber?

Lady Macbeth   Donalbain.

Macbeth
[*Looking at his hands*] This is a sorry sight.

Lady Macbeth
A foolish thought to say a sorry sight.

Lady Macbeth (handwritten, top)

Macbeth
There's one did laugh in 's sleep, and one cried
  'Murder!'
That they did wake each other: I stood and heard
  them;
25 But they did say their prayers, and address'd them
Again to sleep.
  Lady Macbeth
                         There are two lodg'd together.
  Macbeth
One cried 'God bless us!', and 'Amen' the other,
As they had seen me with these hangman's hands.
Listening their fear, I could not say 'Amen',
30 When they did say 'God bless us!'
  Lady Macbeth   Consider it not so deeply.
  Macbeth
But wherefore could not I pronounce 'Amen'?
I had most need of blessing, and 'Amen'
Stuck in my throat.
  Lady Macbeth These deeds must not be thought
After these ways; so, it will make us mad.
  Macbeth
35 Methought I heard a voice cry 'Sleep no more!
Macbeth does murder sleep'—the innocent sleep,
Sleep that knits up the ravell'd sleave of care,
The death of each day's life, sore labour's bath,
Balm of hurt minds, great nature's second course,
40 Chief nourisher in life's feast—
  Lady Macbeth   What do you mean?
  Macbeth
Still it cried, 'Sleep no more!' to all the house:
'Glamis hath murder'd sleep, and therefore Cawdor
Shall sleep no more, Macbeth shall sleep no more!'
  Lady Macbeth
Who was it that thus cried? Why, worthy thane,
45 You do unbend your noble strength to think
So brainsickly of things. Go, get some water,
And wash this filthy witness from your hand.
Why did you bring these daggers from the place?

25   _address'd them_ : prepared
themselves.

26   _lodg'd_ : housed.

28   _As_ : as if.
      hangman. The hangman drew the
entrails from his victims, and cut them
into quarters, after hanging them.
Therefore his hands were covered in
blood.
29   _Listening_ : listening to.

Robotic Macbeth controlled by Lady Mac (handwritten)

37   _knits up_ : smooths out, pieces
together.
      ravell'd : tangled.
      sleave : skein (of wool or silk).
39   _Balm_ : soothing ointment.
39–40 _second course . . . feast_. The main
dish ('Chief nourisher') at a feast was
the 'second course'. Even today the
English eat soup or some small fish
dish before the main dish of meat.

45   _unbend_ : relax (his strength had
previously been bent like a bow).
46   _brainsickly_ : deliriously.
47   _witness_ : evidence.

They must lie there: go, carry them, and smear
50 The sleepy grooms with blood.
       Macbeth   I'll go no more:
I am afraid to think what I have done;
Look on 't again I dare not.
       Lady Macbeth   Infirm of purpose!
Give me the daggers. The sleeping and the dead
Are but as pictures; 'tis the eye of childhood
55 That fears a painted devil. If he do bleed,
I'll gild the faces of the grooms withal;
For it must seem their guilt.
          [*Exit. Someone knocks at the gate*

       Macbeth   Whence is that knocking?
How is 't with me, when every noise appals me?
What hands are here! Ha! they pluck out mine eyes.
60 Will all great Neptune's ocean wash this blood
Clean from my hand? No, this my hand will rather
The multitudinous seas incarnadine,
Making the green one red.

       Enter Lady Macbeth
       Lady Macbeth
My hands are of your colour, but I shame
65 To wear a heart so white. [*Knocking*] I hear a
    knocking
At the south entry; retire we to our chamber;
A little water clears us of this deed;
How easy is it, then! Your constancy
Hath left you unattended. [*Knocking*] Hark! more
    knocking.
70 Get on your night-gown, lest occasion call us,
And show us to be watchers. Be not lost
So poorly in your thoughts.
       Macbeth
To know my deed 'twere best not know myself.
                [*Knocking*
Wake Duncan with thy knocking! I would thou
    couldst!   [*Exeunt*

55   *a painted devil :* a picture of a devil.

57   *guilt.* Lady Macbeth makes a cruel pun here on *guilt* and *gilt.*

59   *they pluck out mine eyes.* Macbeth's eyes are almost falling out of his head at the sight of his bloody hands.

62   *multitudinous :* very great in number.
incarnadine : dye scarlet (see
Introduction, p. viii).

68–9   Your strength of mind has deserted you.

70   *lest occasion call us :* in case there is need to call for us.
71   *watchers :* still awake, not in bed.
72   *poorly :* feebly.

73   If I must recognize what I have done, it would be better that I did not recognize myself (because the deed is damnable, and he would have to condemn himself).
74   *I would thou couldst :* I wish you could.

Act 2   scene 3

All is discovered. The Porter is roused from his drunken sleep by Macduff and Lennox. They go to call upon the king but find that he has been murdered. Macbeth panics and kills Duncan's attendants, explaining that he did this from a sense of outraged loyalty and grief. Duncan's two sons are afraid for their own safety, and slip away secretly.

2   *have old* : have plenty of.

4   *Beelzebub* : one of the chief devils.

4-5 *farmer . . . plenty* : the farmer had hoarded his corn, hoping for a famine when the price of corn would rise; hearing that the harvests were good (and the price would fall) he hanged himself.

6   *time-server* : one who changes his opinions to suit the times.

     napkins : handkerchiefs.

8   *the other devil*. The Porter cannot remember the name of another devil.

9   *equivocator* : double-dealer, one who avoids telling the truth without actually telling a lie.

     the scales : the scales held by the statue of Justice.

13-14 *English tailor . . . French hose* : the

Scene 3 *The courtyard of Macbeth's castle*

Knocking. Enter a Porter

Porter

Here's a knocking, indeed! If a man were porter of hell-gate, he should have old turning the key. [*Knocking*] Knock, knock, knock! Who's there, i' the name of Beelzebub? Here's a farmer that

5 hanged himself on the expectation of plenty : come in time-server; have napkins enough about you; here you'll sweat for 't. [*Knocking*] Knock, knock! Who's there, i' the other devil's name! Faith, here's an equivocator, that could swear in both the scales

10 against either scale; who committed treason enough for God's sake, yet could not equivocate to heaven : O! come in, equivocator. [*Knocking*] Knock, knock, knock! Who's there? Faith, here's an English tailor come hither for stealing out of a French hose :

15 come in, tailor; here you may roast your goose. [*Knocking*] Knock, knock; never at quiet! What are you? But this place is too cold for hell. I'll devil-porter it no further : I had thought to have let in some of all professions, that go the primrose

20 way to the everlasting bonfire. [*Knocking*] Anon, anon! I pray you, remember the porter.

[*Opens the gate*

tailor had tried to steal material when he was making tight-fitting breeches ('French hose'), and so made them too tight, and was caught.

15   *roast your goose* : the 'goose' was a tailor's flat-iron.

19-20   *primrose way* : easy path; the 'primrose' is a delicate, yellow, spring flower.

20   *everlasting bonfire* : hell.

20-1   *Anon, anon* : I'm coming.

21   *remember the porter* : tip the porter for opening the gate.

23   *lie so late* : sleep so late.

24   *carousing* : drinking.
    second cock : second cock-crow, well after dawn.

27   *Marry* : by the Virgin Mary (but the oath was so common that it means no more than 'indeed').
    nose-painting : it makes the nose red.

28-36   'Drink is a double-dealer ("equivocator") so far as lechery is concerned, because it makes a man feel virile, but at the same time renders him impotent ("mars him").' The Porter repeats this idea, in different words, three times, then concludes that drink cheats a man with a dream, lies to him (and makes him lie down), and leaves him.

38   *i' the very throat* : a direct lie (not an equivocation).
    on me : of me.

39   *requited* : paid him back.

40   *he took up my legs* : I fell down.

41   *made a shift* : contrived.
    to cast : to throw him down (by urinating).

42   *stirring* : awake.

46   *timely* : early.

47   *slipp'd the hour* : missed the time.

Enter Macduff *and* Lennox

Macduff
Was it so late, friend, ere you went to bed, that you do lie so late?

Porter
Faith, sir, we were carousing till the second cock; 25 and drink, sir, is a great provoker of three things.

Macduff
What three things does drink especially provoke?

Porter
Marry, sir, nose-painting, sleep, and urine. Lechery, sir, it provokes, and unprovokes: it provokes the desire, but it takes away the per-30 formance. Therefore, much drink may be said to be an equivocator with lechery: it makes him, and it mars him; it sets him on, and it takes him off; it persuades him, and disheartens him; makes him stand to, and not stand to: in conclusion, 35 equivocates him in a sleep, and, giving him the lie, leaves him.

Macduff
I believe drink gave thee the lie last night.

Porter
That it did, sir; i' the very throat on me: but I requited him for his lie, and (I think) being too 40 strong for him, though he took up my legs some-time, yet I made a shift to cast him.

Macduff
Is thy master stirring?

Enter Macbeth
Our knocking has awak'd him; here he comes.

Lennox
Good morrow, noble sir.

Macbeth   Good morrow, both.

Macduff
45 Is the king stirring, worthy thane?

Macbeth   Not yet.

Macduff
He did command me to call timely on him: I have almost slipp'd the hour.

Macbeth   I'll bring you to him.

Macduff

I know this is a joyful trouble to you;
But yet 'tis one.

Macbeth

50 The labour we delight in physics pain.
This is the door.

Macduff   I'll make so bold to call,
For 'tis my limited service.   [*Exit*

Lennox

Goes the king hence to-day?

Macbeth   He does: he did appoint so.

Lennox

The night has been unruly: where we lay,
55 Our chimneys were blown down; and, as they say,
Lamentings heard i' the air; strange screams of
    death,
And prophesying with accents terrible
Of dire combustion and confus'd events
New hatch'd to the woeful time. The obscure bird
60 Clamour'd the livelong night: some say the earth
Was feverous and did shake.

Macbeth   'Twas a rough night.

Lennox

My young remembrance cannot parallel
A fellow to it.

Re-enter Macduff

Macduff

O horror! horror! horror! Tongue nor heart
65 Cannot conceive nor name thee!

Macbeth |
Lennox | What's the matter?

Macduff

Confusion now hath made his masterpiece!
Most sacrilegious murder hath broke ope
The Lord's anointed temple, and stole thence
The life o' the building!

Macbeth

70 What is 't you say? the life?

Lennox

Mean you his majesty?

50   Work that we enjoy cures ('physics')
any trouble ('pain') that it causes us.

52   *limited :* appointed.

58   *dire combustion :* terrible confusion.
59   *hatch'd :* born (as chickens are
'hatched' from eggs).
      woeful time. Lennox refers to the
war with Norway, but his words are
unintentionally apt to describe the
events of the past night.
      obscure bird : owl, the bird of
darkness (obscurity).
60   *livelong :* entire.
62-3 In all my young life I cannot
remember a night like this.

66   *Confusion :* chaos.
67   *sacrilegious :* unholy.
      ope : open.
68   *anointed.* When he was crowned
king, Duncan would have been
anointed with holy oil, to signify that
he was God's deputy on earth.

73   *Gorgon.* In Greek mythology the Gorgon Medusa, a monster with snakes instead of hair, turned every man to stone who looked on her. The sight of Duncan's murdered body will have the same effect.

77-81   Macduff calls on everyone to wake from sleep, which is an imitation ('counterfeit') of death, to look at the real thing, and to rise up like ghosts ('sprites') from their graves to come face to face ('countenance') with this horror, as terrible as a picture of the Last Judgement ('great doom').

77   *downy*: comfortable (because their pillows would be stuffed with 'down', the soft feathers of ducks and geese).

83   *calls to parley*: summons to a discussion.

86-7   To repeat this matter to a woman would kill her as she heard it.

92   *before this chance*: before this happened.

94   *nothing serious in mortality*: nothing important in life.

95   *toys*: trifles.

96-7   Macbeth compares the earth to a wine-cellar ('vault') from which the best wine has been drawn, so that it can now boast ('brag') only of the dregs ('lees').

Macduff
Approach the chamber, and destroy your sight
With a new Gorgon: do not bid me speak;
See, and then speak yourselves.
                              [*Exeunt* Macbeth *and* Lennox
                                        Awake! awake!
75 Ring the alarum-bell. Murder and treason!
Banquo and Donalbain! Malcolm, awake!
Shake off this downy sleep, death's counterfeit,
And look on death itself! Up, up, and see
The great doom's image! Malcolm! Banquo!
80 As from your graves rise up, and walk like sprites,
To countenance this horror! Ring the bell.
                                        [*Bell rings*

                    Enter Lady Macbeth
Lady Macbeth
What's the business,
That such a hideous trumpet calls to parley
The sleepers of the house? Speak, speak!
            Macduff   O gentle lady!
85 'Tis not for you to hear what I can speak;
The repetition in a woman's ear
Would murder as it fell.

                    Enter Banquo
                                    O Banquo! Banquo!
Our royal master's murder'd!
            Lady Macbeth   Woe, alas!
What! in our house?
            Banquo   Too cruel anywhere.
90 Dear Duff, I prithee, contradict thyself,
And say it is not so.

                    Enter Macbeth *and* Lennox
            Macbeth
Had I but died an hour before this chance,
I had liv'd a blessed time; for, from this instant,
There 's nothing serious in mortality,
95 All is but toys; renown and grace is dead,
The wine of life is drawn, and the mere lees
Is left this vault to brag of.

Enter Malcolm *and* Donalbain

Donalbain
What is amiss?

Macbeth   You are, and do not know 't:
The spring, the head, the fountain of your blood
100 Is stopp'd; the very source of it is stopp'd.

Macduff
Your royal father's murder'd.

Malcolm   O! by whom?

Lennox
Those of his chamber, as it seem'd, had done 't:
Their hands and faces were all badg'd with blood;
So were their daggers, which unwip'd we found
105 Upon their pillows: they star'd, and were distracted;
No man's life was to be trusted with them.

Macbeth
O yet I do repent me of my fury,
That I did kill them.

Macduff   Wherefore did you so?

Macbeth
Who can be wise, amaz'd, temperate and furious,
110 Loyal and neutral, in a moment? No man.
The expedition of my violent love
Outran the pauser, reason. Here lay Duncan,
His silver skin lac'd with his golden blood;
And his gash'd stabs look'd like a breach in nature
115 For ruin's wasteful entrance: there, the murderers,
Steep'd in the colours of their trade, their daggers
Unmannerly breech'd with gore: who could refrain,
That had a heart to love, and in that heart
Courage to make 's love known?

Lady Macbeth   Help me hence, ho!

Macduff
120 Look to the lady.

Malcolm
[*Aside to* Donalbain] Why do we hold our tongues,
That most may claim this argument for ours?

Donalbain
[*Aside to* Malcolm] What should be spoken
Here where our fate, hid in an auger-hole,
May rush and seize us? Let's away: our tears
125 Are not yet brew'd.

98   *amiss :* wrong.

103   *badg'd :* wearing the badges of their
profession (as murderers).

111   *expedition :* speed.
112   *pauser :* delayer, that which makes
one stop and think.
114-15 Duncan's wounds were like
openings in his body where destruction
('ruin') had forced an entrance to lay
waste his life.
116   Macbeth repeats Lennox's
thought (line 103), that the servants
were wearing the coloured uniforms of
their trade as murderers.
steep'd : dyed.
117   *Unmannerly :* indecently.
breech'd : clothed (in breeches).
refrain : stop himself from acting.
121   *argument :* topic of discussion.
122-4   What can we say here, where our
fate (death) may be hiding in some tiny
hole, ready to rush upon and seize us?
(An auger is a sharp-pointed tool for
boring holes in wood.)

125   *brew'd :* ready to flow (tea is said
to be 'brewed' when it is ready to
drink).

126   *Upon the foot of motion* : ready to
      move—to express itself either in words
      or in actions.
127-8 When we have dressed our weak
      (because unclothed) bodies, so that we
      don't catch cold from exposure.
129   *question* : investigate.
130   *scruples* : doubts.
131   *In the great hand of God* : in
      God's great protection.
132   *undivulg'd pretence* : hidden
      design.

134   *briefly* : quickly.
      manly readiness : proper clothing
      (and also, perhaps, determination).

136   *consort* : mix.
137   *office* : duty.
138   *easy* : easily.

141-2 The closer we are in relationship
      ('in blood') to the king, the more likely
      we are to be murdered.
142   *shaft* : arrow.
143   *lighted* : alighted, found its mark.
144   *avoid the aim* : keep out of its way.
145   *dainty of leave-taking* : fussy about
      saying a formal goodbye.
146   *shift away* : steal away.
146-7 It is a justifiable theft, to steal
      (oneself) away from a place where
      there is no mercy.

Malcolm
[*Aside to* Donalbain] Nor our strong sorrow
Upon the foot of motion.
          Banquo   Look to the lady:
                              [Lady Macbeth *is carried out*
And when we have our naked frailties hid,
That suffer in exposure, let us meet,
And question this most bloody piece of work,
130 To know it further. Fears and scruples shake us:
In the great hand of God I stand, and thence
Against the undivulg'd pretence I fight
Of treasonous malice.
          Macduff   And so do I.
          All   So all.
          Macbeth
Let's briefly put on manly readiness,
135 And meet i' the hall together.
          All   Well contented.
                    [*Exeunt all but* Malcolm *and* Donalbain
          Malcolm
What will you do? Let's not consort with them:
To show an unfelt sorrow is an office
Which the false man does easy. I'll to England.
          Donalbain
To Ireland, I; our separated fortune
140 Shall keep us both the safer: where we are,
There's daggers in men's smiles: the near in blood,
The nearer bloody.
          Malcolm   This murderous shaft that's shot
Hath not yet lighted, and our safest way
Is to avoid the aim: therefore, to horse;
145 And let us not be dainty of leave-taking,
But shift away: there's warrant in that theft
Which steals itself when there's no mercy left.
                                        [*Exeunt*

Act 2   scene 4

Ross and an Old Man discuss the unnatural events that occurred on the night of Duncan's murder. They learn from Macduff that the king's two sons have fled, and that because of this they are suspected of having bribed their father's servants to murder him. Macduff also tells them that Macbeth has been chosen as king, and that he has gone to Scone for the coronation.

3 *sore :* strange.
4 *trifled former knowings :* made all that I have known before seem trivial.
5 *troubled :* angered.
7 *strangles the travelling lamp :* chokes the sun (with clouds).
8 *predominance :* superior power.
9 *entomb :* bury.

12 *falcon :* a bird of prey, beautiful and fierce.
    pride of place : highest point of the falcon's flight.
13 *mousing :* that catches mice.
    hawk'd : pounced upon from the air, as a hawk (a bird even more powerful than the falcon) catches its prey.

15 *minions of their race :* the best (most favoured) of their breed.
16 *broke their stalls :* broke out of their stables.
17 *Contending 'gainst obedience :* fighting against the training that made them obedient.

Scene 4 *Outside Macbeth's castle*

Enter Ross *and an* Old Man

Old Man
Threescore and ten I can remember well;
Within the volume of which time I have seen
Hours dreadful and things strange, but this sore night
Hath trifled former knowings.
                              Ross   Ah good father,
5 Thou seest the heavens, as troubled with man's act,
Threaten his bloody stage : by the clock 'tis day,
And yet dark night strangles the travelling lamp.
Is 't night's predominance, or the day's shame,
That darkness does the face of earth entomb,
10 When living light should kiss it?
          Old Man   'Tis unnatural,
Even like the deed that's done. On Tuesday last,
A falcon, towering in her pride of place,
Was by a mousing owl hawk'd at and kill'd.
          Ross
And Duncan's horses—a thing most strange and certain—
15 Beauteous and swift, the minions of their race,
Turn'd wild in nature, broke their stalls, flung out,
Contending 'gainst obedience, as they would
Make war with mankind.
          Old Man   'Tis said they ate each other.
          Ross
They did so, to the amazement of mine eyes,
20 That look'd upon 't. Here comes the good Macduff.

[handwritten annotations:] King move powerful than Macbeth   King-eagle   Macbeth owl

Enter Macduff

How goes the world, sir, now?

Macduff   Why, see you not?

Ross

Is 't known who did this more than bloody deed?

Macduff

Those that Macbeth hath slain.

Ross   Alas, the day!

What good could they pretend?

Macduff   They were suborn'd.

25 Malcolm and Donalbain, the king's two sons,
Are stol'n away and fled, which puts upon them
Suspicion of the deed.

Ross   'Gainst nature still!

Thriftless ambition, that wilt ravin up
Thine own life's means! Then 'tis most like

30 The sovereignty will fall upon Macbeth.

Macduff

He is already nam'd, and gone to Scone
To be invested.

Ross   Where is Duncan's body?

Macduff

Carried to Colmekill,
The sacred storehouse of his predecessors

35 And guardian of their bones.

Ross   Will you to Scone?

Macduff

No, cousin, I'll to Fife.

Ross   Well, I will thither.

Macduff

Well, may you see things well done there: adieu!
Lest our old robes sit easier than our new!

Ross

Farewell, father.

Old Man

40 God's benison go with you; and with those
That would make good of bad, and friends of foes!

[*Exeunt*

24 *What . . . pretend* : what good did they
think it would do them?
suborn'd : bribed.

27 *still* : again.

28 *ravin up* : devour.

29 *Thine own life's means* : that which
is necessary to give you life.

30 *sovereignty* : kingship.

31 *nam'd* : elected.
Scone : at one time the capital of
Scotland. (The Stone of Scone, on
which Scottish kings were crowned, is
now kept in Westminster Abbey, and
it is used in British coronation
ceremonies.)

32 *invested* : made king (at a ceremony
where he receives the symbols of
royalty—see illustration, p. 65).

38 *sit* : fit.

40 *benison* : blessing.

Act 3

Banquo suspects Macbeth, but he still hopes that the witches' prophecy may also come true for him. He promises Macbeth that he will return in time for the feast, and then leaves Macbeth alone on the stage. Macbeth reveals his inmost thoughts to us, before the Murderers are brought in, and a new plot is started.

4 The crown would not be passed on to Macbeth's descendants.

7 *shine*: show favour (as the sun shines).

8 *verities . . . good*: truths which have been proved in your case.

9 *my oracles*: prophets for me.

Scene 1 *Forres. A room in the palace*

> *Enter* Banquo

Banquo
Thou hast it now: King, Cawdor, Glamis, all,
As the weird women promis'd; and, I fear,
Thou play'dst most foully for 't; yet it was said
It should not stand in thy posterity,
5 But that myself should be the root and father
Of many kings. If there come truth from them—
As upon thee, Macbeth, their speeches shine—
Why, by the verities on thee made good,
May they not be my oracles as well,
10 And set me up in hope? But, hush! no more.

> *A trumpet sounds. Enter* Macbeth, *as king*;
> Lady Macbeth, *as queen*; Lennox, Ross,
> Lords, Ladies, *and* Attendants

Macbeth
Here's our chief guest.

Lady Macbeth   If he had been forgotten,
It had been as a gap in our great feast,
And all-thing unbecoming.

Macbeth
To-night we hold a solemn supper, sir,
15 And I'll request your presence.

Banquo   Let your highness
Command upon me; to the which my duties
Are with a most indissoluble tie
For ever knit.

14 *solemn supper*: formal dinner.

16 *to the which*: to which command.

17 *indissoluble*: which cannot be broken.

18 *knit*: bound.

Macbeth
Ride you this afternoon?
Banquo
20 Ay, my good lord.
Macbeth
We should have else desir'd your good advice—
Which still hath been both grave and prosperous—
In this day's council; but we'll take to-morrow.
Is 't far you ride?
Banquo
25 As far, my lord, as will fill up the time
'Twixt this and supper; go not my horse the better,
I must become a borrower of the night
For a dark hour or twain.
Macbeth   Fail not our feast.
Banquo
My lord, I will not.
Macbeth
30 We hear our bloody cousins are bestow'd
In England and in Ireland, not confessing
Their cruel parricide, filling their hearers
With strange invention; but of that to-morrow,
When, therewithal, we shall have cause of state
35 Craving us jointly. Hie you to horse; adieu
Till you return at night. Goes Fleance with you?
Banquo
Ay, my good lord: our time does call upon 's.
Macbeth
I wish your horses swift and sure of foot;
And so I do commend you to their backs.
40 Farewell.   [*Exit* Banquo
Let every man be master of his time
Till seven at night; to make society
The sweeter welcome, we will keep ourself
Till supper-time alone; while then, God be with
    you!
        [*Exeunt all but* Macbeth *and an* Attendant
45 Sirrah, a word with you. Attend those men
Our pleasure?
Attendant
They are, my lord, without the palace gate.

22   *still* : always.
    grave : serious.
    prosperous : profitable.

26   *this* : this time.
26-8 If my horse does not go faster than
    I expect, I shall have to use one or two
    ('twain') hours of darkness from the
    night.

30   *bloody* : stained with the blood of
    Duncan.
    bestow'd : settled.

33   *strange invention* : strange tales
    which they have invented.
33-5 We will talk more of that tomorrow,
    when there will also be affairs of state,
    that demand the attention of both of us.

37   *our time does call upon 's* : it is time
    for us to go.

41   *master of his time* : use his time as
    he wishes.

47   *without* : outside.

48-9   It is nothing to be as I am now (i.e. king); I must be king in safety.

50   *stick deep* : are deeply rooted.
royalty of nature : nobility of character.

51   *that . . . fear'd* : that which Macbeth ought to be afraid of.

52   *temper* : courage, spirit.

55   *being* : existence.

56-7   Macbeth's guiding spirit ('genius') is made timid by Banquo's—just as the Roman Mark Antony's spirit was said (by Plutarch) to be subdued by Julius Caesar's.

57   *chid* : reproached.

61-2   The witches gave Macbeth a crown and sceptre, but without the promise that his descendants would inherit them.

62   *gripe* : grasp.

63   *an unlineal hand* : a hand that does not belong to any of my descendants.

65   *fil'd* : defiled.

67   *rancours* : bitternesses.

68   *eternal jewel* : i.e. his immortal soul.

69   *common enemy of man* : i.e. Satan, who is the enemy of all men in general (in 'common'), not of one man in particular.

71-2   Macbeth calls upon Fate to come as a knight to tournament ('the list') to fight as a champion against him, to the death ('utterance' = utmost).

77   *he* : i.e. Banquo.

78   *under fortune* : below what you deserved.

80   *pass'd in probation* : demonstrated to you.

81   *borne in hand* : deceived.
cross'd : thwarted.
instruments : the means used.

Macbeth
Bring them before us. [*Exit* Attendant] To be thus
    is nothing;
But to be safely thus. Our fears in Banquo
50 Stick deep, and in his royalty of nature
Reigns that which would be fear'd: 'tis much he
    dares,
And, to that dauntless temper of his mind,
He hath a wisdom that doth guide his valour
To act in safety. There is none but he
55 Whose being I do fear; and under him
My genius is rebuk'd, as, it is said,
Mark Antony's was by Caesar. He chid the sisters
When first they put the name of king upon me,
And bade them speak to him; then, prophet-like,
60 They hail'd him father to a line of kings.
Upon my head they plac'd a fruitless crown,
And put a barren sceptre in my gripe,
Thence to be wrench'd with an unlineal hand,
No son of mine succeeding. If 't be so,
65 For Banquo's issue have I fil'd my mind;
For them the gracious Duncan have I murder'd;
Put rancours in the vessel of my peace
Only for them; and mine eternal jewel
Given to the common enemy of man,
70 To make them kings, the seed of Banquo kings!
Rather than so, come fate into the list,
And champion me to th' utterance! Who's there?

Enter Attendant, *with two* Murderers
Now go to the door, and stay there till we call.
                              [*Exit* Attendant
Was it not yesterday we spoke together?
    First Murderer
75 It was, so please your highness.
    Macbeth   Well then, now
Have you consider'd of my speeches? Know
That it was he, in the times past, which held you
So under fortune, which you thought had been
Our innocent self. This I made good to you
80 In our last conference, pass'd in probation with
    you,
How you were borne in hand, how cross'd, the
    instruments,

82   *wrought* : worked.

83   *half a soul* : a half-wit.
           notion craz'd : the mind of a
madman.

86-8   Is patience so much the strongest
         of all your qualities that you will
         endure this?
88   *gospell'd* : filled with the teaching
         of the Christian Gospels.
89   *this good man.* Macbeth is being
ironic.
           issue : descendants.
91   *yours* : your descendants.

92-101   In the general list of natural
         beings they are classified as 'men', just
         as there are different breeds of dog
         which are all included under 'dog'.
         But the really valuable list ('file') is
         that which notes the precise qualities
         of every animal, according to its
         natural gifts. This list which notes
         special qualities ('Particular addition')
         is distinct from the list ('bill') that
         counts them all the same. This is true
         of men, just as it is of dogs.
94   *Shoughs* : shaggy dogs.
           water-rugs : rough-haired water
dogs.
           demi-wolves : cross-breeds: half-
wolf, half-dog.
           clept : called.
97   *housekeeper* : guard-dog.
102   *station* : position.
104-5   I will tell you secretly ('in your
         bosoms') of a plan which, when it is
         carried out, will remove your enemy.
106   Fasten you firmly to my heart
         and love.
107-8   Macbeth can only be sick whilst
         Banquo is alive, but if Banquo were
         dead, he would be perfectly healthy.
109   *buffets* : misfortunes.
110   *incens'd* : angered.
112   *tugg'd with* : dragged about by.
113-14   I would risk my life on any
         gamble, where I could either improve
         it or lose it.

Who wrought with them, and all things else that
        might
To half a soul and to a notion craz'd
Say, 'Thus did Banquo.'
                First Murderer   You made it known to us.
Macbeth
85 I did so; and went further, which is now
Our point of second meeting. Do you find
Your patience so predominant in your nature
That you can let this go? Are you so gospell'd
To pray for this good man and for his issue,
90 Whose heavy hand hath bow'd you to the grave
And beggar'd yours for ever?
                First Murderer   We are men, my liege.
Macbeth
Ay, in the catalogue ye go for men;
As hounds and greyhounds, mongrels, spaniels,
        curs,
Shoughs, water-rugs, and demi-wolves, are clept
95 All by the name of dogs: the valu'd file
Distinguishes the swift, the slow, the subtle,
The housekeeper, the hunter, every one
According to the gift which bounteous nature
Hath in him clos'd; whereby he does receive
100 Particular addition, from the bill
That writes them all alike: and so of men.
Now, if you have a station in the file,
Not i' the worst rank of manhood, say it;
And I will put that business in your bosoms,
105 Whose execution takes your enemy off,
Grapples you to the heart and love of us,
Who wear our health but sickly in his life,
Which in his death were perfect.
                Second Murderer   I am one, my liege,
Whom the vile blows and buffets of the world
110 Have so incens'd that I am reckless what
I do to spite the world.
                First Murderer   And I another,
So weary with disasters, tugg'd with fortune,
That I would set my life on any chance,
To mend it or be rid on 't.

Macbeth   Both of you
115 Know Banquo was your enemy.
    Second Murderer   True, my lord.
    Macbeth
So is he mine; and in such bloody distance
That every minute of his being thrusts
Against my near'st of life: and though I could
With bare-fac'd power sweep him from my sight
120 And bid my will avouch it, yet I must not,
For certain friends that are both his and mine,
Whose loves I may not drop, but wail his fall
Who I myself struck down; and thence it is
That I to your assistance do make love,
125 Masking the business from the common eye
For sundry weighty reasons.
    Second Murderer   We shall, my lord,
Perform what you command us.
    First Murderer   Though our lives—
    Macbeth
Your spirits shine through you. Within this hour
    at most
I will advise you where to plant yourselves,
130 Acquaint you with the perfect spy o' the time,
The moment on 't; for 't must be done to-night,
And something from the palace; always thought
That I require a clearness: and with him—
To leave no rubs nor botches in the work—
135 Fleance his son, that keeps him company,
Whose absence is no less material to me
Than is his father's, must embrace the fate
Of that dark hour. Resolve yourselves apart;
I'll come to you anon.
    Second Murderer   We are resolv'd, my lord.
    Macbeth
140 I'll call upon you straight: abide within.
                  [*Exeunt* Murderers
It is concluded: Banquo, thy soul's flight,
If it find heaven, must find it out to-night.   [*Exit*

---

116 *bloody distance*: deadly distance ('distance' is a technical term in fencing for the space between two fighters).

117 *thrusts*: i.e. like a fencer's sword.

118 *near'st of life*: vital parts.

119 *bare-fac'd*: openly; Macbeth as king has power to kill Banquo without giving any excuse for his action.

120 *bid my will avouch it*: say I did it because I wanted to.

121 *For*: because.

122 *may not drop*: must not lose.
but wail: instead I must lament.

124 *make love*: make advances.

125 *common eye*: public gaze.

126 *sundry*: various.

129 *plant*: hide.

130 *perfect spy o' the time*: the best time that I can see for the murder.

132 *something from*: at a distance from.
always thought: always have it in your mind.

133 *I require a clearness*: I want to be free from suspicion.

134 *rubs*: mistakes.
botches: bungling.

136 *absence*: death.
material: important.

138 *Resolve yourselves apart*: make up your minds in private.

139 *anon*: immediately.

140 *straight*: straight away, at once.

Act 3   scene 2

Macbeth and his wife are both worried. He tells her that he is going to take some action, but he will not tell her what it is.

3–4   I will wait until he has time to speak to me.

4–7   We have gained nothing, and lost everything, when we are not satisfied by getting what we wanted. It is better to be that which we kill than, as a result of killing, live in an insecure ('doubtful') pleasure.

9–11   Having depressing imagination for your companion, and living with those thoughts that should have died when the subject of them (i.e. Duncan) was killed.

12   *without regard* : ignored.

13–15   Macbeth feels that although he is evil, his evilness is feeble ('poor'), and it is in danger now, just as it was before the death of Duncan, from righteousness, which Macbeth sees as a snake which has been wounded ('scorch'd') but which will heal up ('close').

16   *frame of things* : structure of creation.
disjoint : collapse.
both the worlds : heaven and earth.

21   *on* : in.

25   *foreign levy* : armies gathered (levied) abroad.

Scene 2 *Another room in the palace*

Enter Lady Macbeth *and a* Servant

Lady Macbeth
Is Banquo gone from court?
Servant
Ay, madam, but returns again to-night.
Lady Macbeth
Say to the king, I would attend his leisure
For a few words.
Servant   Madam, I will.   [*Exit*
Lady Macbeth   Nought's had, all's spent,
5 Where our desire is got without content :
'Tis safer to be that which we destroy
Than by destruction dwell in doubtful joy.

Enter Macbeth
How now, my lord! why do you keep alone,
Of sorriest fancies your companions making,
10 Using those thoughts which should indeed have died
With them they think on? Things without all remedy
Should be without regard : what's done is done.
Macbeth
We have scorch'd the snake, not kill'd it :
She'll close and be herself, whilst our poor malice
15 Remains in danger of her former tooth.
But let the frame of things disjoint, both the worlds suffer,
Ere we will eat our meal in fear, and sleep
In the affliction of these terrible dreams
That shake us nightly. Better be with the dead,
20 Whom we, to gain our peace, have sent to peace,
Than on the torture of the mind to lie
In restless ecstasy. Duncan is in his grave ;
After life's fitful fever he sleeps well ;
Treason has done his worst : nor steel, nor poison,
25 Malice domestic, foreign levy, nothing

27   *sleek o'er :* smooth down.
30   Remember Banquo (because she will remember what has been prophesied to him).
31   *Present him eminence :* pay him great respect.
32-3   As long as we are unsafe, we must wash our titles in flattery as though it were a stream (so that the titles of 'king' and 'queen' would seem to be clean and honourable).
34   *vizards :* masks, especially the part of the helmet that covers the face.

38   Nature (or Life) does not hold an eternal copyright on Banquo and Fleance (so that they can never die).
39   *they are assailable :* they can be attacked.
40   *jocund :* joyful.
      bat. The bat is like a mouse with wings, which flies only in the dark; it often lives in old churches with lonely 'cloisters'.
41   *Hecate :* goddess of witches.
42   *beetle.* The beetle flies at night (when men are sleepy—'drowsy'), and makes a humming noise which seems like a curfew bell ('night's . . . peal') rung when men are 'yawning'.
44   *dreadful note :* terrible to hear of.
45   *chuck.* A term of endearment, still used in England in parts of the Midlands.
46   *seeling :* blinding. This is a technical term from hunting; a falcon's eyes were 'seeled' when the eyelids were sewn with thread to make the bird helpless so that it would become tame.
49   *that great bond :* Banquo's life, which Macbeth thinks of as a legal document.

Can touch him further.
  Lady Macbeth   Come on;
Gentle my lord, sleek o'er your rugged looks;
Be bright and jovial among your guests to-night.
  Macbeth
So shall I, love; and so, I pray, be you.
30 Let your remembrance apply to Banquo;
Present him eminence, both with eye and tongue:
Unsafe the while, that we
Must lave our honours in these flattering streams,
And make our faces vizards to our hearts,
35 Disguising what they are.
  Lady Macbeth   You must leave this.
  Macbeth
O full of scorpions is my mind, dear wife;
Thou know'st that Banquo and his Fleance lives.
  Lady Macbeth
But in them nature's copy's not eterne.
  Macbeth
There's comfort yet; they are assailable;
40 Then be thou jocund. Ere the bat hath flown
His cloister'd flight, ere to black Hecate's summons
The shard-born beetle with his drowsy hums
Hath rung night's yawning peal, there shall be done
A deed of dreadful note.
  Lady Macbeth   What's to be done?
  Macbeth
45 Be innocent of the knowledge, dearest chuck,
Till thou applaud the deed. Come, seeling night,
Scarf up the tender eye of pitiful day,
And with thy bloody and invisible hand
Cancel and tear to pieces that great bond

50   *keeps me pale :* keeps me fenced in.
The 'pale' was the boundary dividing
one country's land from another's.
    crow : a large and ugly black bird,
similar to the 'rook'.
53   The wicked beings that work in the
night become alert in hunting their
prey.
55   Deeds that are started with evil
grow stronger with more evil.

Act 3   scene 3
A third murderer appears unexpectedly,
and helps to murder Banquo.

2   *He . . . mistrust :* there is no need for
him to mistrust us.
2–3   *delivers Our offices :* tells us our
duties.
4   *To the direction just :* to the last
detail.
6   *lated :* belated.
7   *To . . . inn :* to get to the inn in time
(before dark).
8   *subject of our watch :* the man we are
watching for.

10   *note of expectation :* the list of guests
expected (for the banquet).

11   *go about :* go a long way round. After
a long journey the horses would be
sweating, and it would be necessary
for the grooms (called by Banquo in
line 9) to walk with them until they
were cool.

50 Which keeps me pale! Light thickens, and the crow
Makes wing to the rooky wood;
Good things of day begin to droop and drowse,
Whiles night's black agents to their preys do rouse.
Thou marvell'st at my words: but hold thee still;
55 Things bad begun make strong themselves by ill:
So, prithee, go with me.   [*Exeunt*

Scene 3 *A park, with a road leading to the palace*

Enter three Murderers
    First Murderer
But who did bid thee join with us?
    Third Murderer   Macbeth.
    Second Murderer
He needs not our mistrust, since he delivers
Our offices and what we have to do
To the direction just.
    First Murderer   Then stand with us.
5   The west yet glimmers with some streaks of day:
Now spurs the lated traveller apace
To gain the timely inn; and near approaches
The subject of our watch.
    Third Murderer   Hark! I hear horses.
    Banquo
[*Offstage*] Give us a light there, ho!
    Second Murderer   Then 'tis he: the rest
10 That are within the note of expectation
Already are i' the court.
    First Murderer   His horses go about.
    Third Murderer
Almost a mile; but he does usually,
So all men do, from hence to the palace gate
Make it their walk.
    Second Murderer
A light, a light!
    Third Murderer   'Tis he.
    First Murderer
15 Stand to 't.

Enter Banquo *and* Fleance, *with a torch*

Banquo

It will be rain to-night.

    First Murderer   Let it come down.

                                  [*They attack* Banquo

Banquo

O, treachery! Fly, good Fleance, fly, fly, fly!

Thou mayst revenge. O slave!

                                [*Dies.* Fleance *escapes*

    Third Murderer

Who did strike out the light?

    First Murderer   Was 't not the way?

    Third Murderer

20 There's but one down; the son is fled.

    Second Murderer   We have lost

Best half of our affair.

    First Murderer

Well, let's away, and say how much is done.

                                    [*Exeunt*

Act 3   scene 4

Macbeth and his wife welcome the guests to their state banquet. The Ghost of Banquo appears, but only Macbeth can see it. Lady Macbeth and the other guests are startled by Macbeth's strange behaviour.

1   *degrees :* social ranks (which would determine the order in which the guests should sit).

3   *society :* the company.

5   *keeps her state :* remains seated on the throne of state.
    in best time : at the right moment.

6   *require her welcome :* request her to welcome you.

Scene 4 *The banqueting hall in the palace*

    Enter Macbeth, Lady Macbeth, Ross,
    Lennox, Lords, *and* Attendants.

    Macbeth

You know your own degrees; sit down: at first and last,

The hearty welcome.

    Lords   Thanks to your majesty.

    Macbeth

Ourself will mingle with society

And play the humble host.

5 Our hostess keeps her state, but in best time

We will require her welcome.

    Lady Macbeth

Pronounce it for me, sir, to all our friends;

For my heart speaks they are welcome.

9   *encounter* : greet.

10   *Both sides are even* : there are equal
     numbers of people sitting on each side
     of the table.

11   *Be large in mirth* : enjoy yourselves
     fully.
     anon : presently.
     measure. A cup of wine would be
     passed round the table, and each man
     would drink from it.

15   *dispatch'd* : dealt with (i.e. killed).

18   *the like* : the same.

19   *the nonpareil* : the best, without an
     equal.

21   *fit* : spasm of fear.
     else : otherwise.
     perfect : completely safe.

22-3 Solid as marble, firm as a rock, as
      free and unconfined as the air
      surrounding us.

24   *cabin'd, cribb'd* : shut up as if in a
     small cabin or hut.

25   *saucy* : intruding.

27   *trenched* : hacked.

28   The smallest of the wounds would
     cause a man's death.

30-1 It will by nature grow into a
      poisonous snake, but is not dangerous
      at present.

32   *hear ourselves* : talk together.

33   *give the cheer* : entertain people (as
     a host should do).

33-5 *the feast . . . welcome*. A banquet is
      no better than a meal that is sold
      unless, during the course of the
      banquet ('while 'tis a-making'), the
      guests are often told by the host how
      welcome they are.

35-7 Eating is best at home, but away
      from home the courtesies of a formal
      occasion give the food an extra sauce;
      without this 'sauce' of ceremony, a
      gathering of people for a meal would
      be poor. Lady Macbeth makes a pun
      on 'meat' and 'meet'.

Enter first Murderer

Macbeth
See, they encounter thee with their hearts' thanks;

10 Both sides are even: here I'll sit i' the midst:
    Be large in mirth; anon, we'll drink a measure
    The table round. [*He goes to the door*] There's blood
        upon thy face.

Murderer
'Tis Banquo's, then.

Macbeth
'Tis better thee without than he within.

15 Is he dispatch'd?

Murderer
My lord, his throat is cut; that I did for him.

Macbeth
Thou art the best o' the cut-throats; yet he's good
That did the like for Fleance: if thou didst it,
Thou art the nonpareil.

Murderer   Most royal sir,

20 Fleance is 'scap'd.

Macbeth
Then comes my fit again: I had else been perfect;
Whole as the marble, founded as the rock,
As broad and general as the casing air:
But now I am cabin'd, cribb'd, confin'd, bound in

25 To saucy doubts and fears. But Banquo's safe?

Murderer
Ay, my good lord; safe in a ditch he bides,
With twenty trenched gashes on his head,
The least a death to nature.

Macbeth   Thanks for that.
There the grown serpent lies: the worm that's fled
30 Hath nature that in time will venom breed,
No teeth for the present. Get thee gone; to-morrow
We'll hear ourselves again.   [*Exit* Murderer

Lady Macbeth   My royal lord,
You do not give the cheer: the feast is sold
That is not often vouch'd, while 'tis a-making,
35 'Tis given with welcome: to feed were best at home;

From thence, the sauce to meat is ceremony;
Meeting were bare without it.

Macbeth   Sweet remembrancer!
Now good digestion wait on appetite,
And health on both!

Lennox   May it please your highness sit?

> *The* Ghost *of* Banquo *enters, and sits in*
> Macbeth's *place*

Macbeth

40 Here had we now our country's honour roof'd,
Were the grac'd person of our Banquo present;
Who may I rather challenge for unkindness
Than pity for mischance!

Ross   His absence, sir,
Lays blame upon his promise. Please 't your highness

45 To grace us with your royal company?

Macbeth
The table 's full.

Lennox   Here is a place reserv'd, sir.

Macbeth
Where?

Lennox
Here, my good lord. What is 't that moves your
highness?

Macbeth
Which of you have done this?

Lords   What, my good lord?

Macbeth

50 Thou canst not say I did it: never shake
Thy gory locks at me.

Ross
Gentlemen, rise; his highness is not well.

Lady Macbeth
Sit, worthy friends: my lord is often thus,
And hath been from his youth: pray you, keep seat;

55 The fit is momentary; upon a thought
He will again be well. If much you note him,

---

37   *remembrancer :* reminder (this may
mean either Lady Macbeth, or the
words she has spoken).

40   *country's honour :* the nobility of the
land.
roof'd : complete (as a house is
completed when the roof is put on).
42   *challenge for unkindness :* rebuke for
lack of courtesy.
43–4   *His . . . promise :* by not being
present, he is at fault for promising to
come.
44   *Please 't :* may it please.

47   *Where?* Only Macbeth can see the
Ghost.

55   *upon a thought :* as fast as you can
think it.
56   *note :* take notice of.

You shall offend him and extend his passion:
Feed, and regard him not. [*Aside to* Macbeth] Are
      you a man?

Macbeth
Ay, and a bold one, that dare look on that
60 Which might appal the devil.

Lady Macbeth   O proper stuff!
This is the very painting of your fear;
This is the air-drawn dagger which, you said,
Led you to Duncan. O these flaws and starts—
Impostors to true fear—would well become
65 A woman's story at a winter's fire,
Authoriz'd by her grandam. Shame itself!
Why do you make such faces? When all's done,
You look but on a stool.

Macbeth
Prithee, see there! behold! look! lo! how say you?
70 Why, what care I? If thou canst nod, speak too.
If charnel-houses and our graves must send
Those that we bury back, our monuments
Shall be the maws of kites.   [Ghost *disappears*

Lady Macbeth What! quite unmann'd in folly?

Macbeth
If I stand here, I saw him.

Lady Macbeth   Fie, for shame!

Macbeth
75 Blood hath been shed ere now, i' the olden time,
Ere human statute purg'd the gentle weal;
Ay, and since too, murders have been perform'd
Too terrible for the ear: the times have been,
That, when the brains were out, the man would die,
80 And there an end; but now they rise again,
With twenty mortal murders on their crowns,
And push us from our stools: this is more strange
Than such a murder is.

Lady Macbeth   My worthy lord,
Your noble friends do lack you.

Macbeth   I do forget.

60   *O proper stuff*: Oh rubbish!
61   *This . . . fear*: this is indeed only
pictured for you by your fear.
62   *air-drawn*: drawn in the air.
63   *flaws and starts*: outbursts and
alarms.

66   *grandam*: grandmother.

71-3   If tombs ('charnel-houses') and
graves allow the dead to return to life,
we shall be forced to use as tombs
('monuments') the stomachs ('maws')
of birds of prey ('kites').
73   *quite . . . folly*: has your foolishness
made you completely forget that you
are a man?

75-80 Once upon a time, before man's
laws made the country ('weal') civilized
('gentle'), there was bloodshed; and
since then, too, there have been
dreadful murders. But in those days,
when his brains had been knocked out,
a man would die, and that was the end
of it.
81   *mortal murders*: fatal wounds.
      crowns: heads.

85   *muse :* wonder.

91-2   To all of you, and to Banquo,
I will drink a toast, and we will all
drink to each other.

92   *the pledge :* the oath of allegiance
to the king.

93   *Avaunt :* Away!

95   *speculation :* intelligent sight.

97   *thing of custom :* regular
occurrence.

101   *arm'd :* i.e. with thick skin and
a tusk, like armour and a sword.
Hyrcan tiger. Tigers of Hircania
(in Persia) were very fierce.

104   *dare :* challenge.

105   *If . . . then :* if I live in fear and
trembling then.
protest : proclaim.

106   *baby of a girl :* baby girl.

109   *displac'd :* upset.

112-13   *You . . . owe :* you make me feel
like a stranger to my own nature.

85 Do not muse at me, my most worthy friends;
I have a strange infirmity, which is nothing
To those that know me. Come, love and health
        to all;
Then, I'll sit down. Give me some wine; fill full.
I drink to the general joy of the whole table,
90 And to our dear friend Banquo, whom we miss;
Would he were here! to all, and him, we thirst,
And all to all.
        Lords   Our duties, and the pledge.
        Enter Ghost
        Macbeth
Avaunt! and quit my sight! Let the earth hide thee!
Thy bones are marrowless, thy blood is cold;
95 Thou hast no speculation in those eyes
Which thou dost glare with.
        Lady Macbeth   Think of this, good peers,
But as a thing of custom: 'tis no other;
Only it spoils the pleasure of the time.
        Macbeth
What man dare, I dare:
100 Approach thou like the rugged Russian bear,
The arm'd rhinoceros, or the Hyrcan tiger;
Take any shape but that, and my firm nerves
Shall never tremble: or be alive again,
And dare me to the desert with thy sword;
105 If trembling I inhabit then, protest me
The baby of a girl. Hence, horrible shadow!
Unreal mockery, hence!   [Ghost *vanishes*
                Why, so; being gone,
I am a man again. Pray you, sit still.
        Lady Macbeth
You have displac'd the mirth, broke the good
        meeting,
110 With most admir'd disorder.
        Macbeth   Can such things be
And overcome us like a summer's cloud,
Without our special wonder? You make me strange
Even to the disposition that I owe,

When now I think you can behold such sights,
115 And keep the natural ruby of your cheeks,
When mine is blanch'd with fear.

Ross   What sights, my lord?

Lady Macbeth
I pray you, speak not; he grows worse and worse;
Question enrages him. At once, good-night:
Stand not upon the order of your going,
120 But go at once.

Lennox   Good-night; and better health
Attend his majesty!

Lady Macbeth   A kind good-night to all!
                        [*Exeunt* Lords *and* Attendants

Macbeth
It will have blood, they say; blood will have blood:
Stones have been known to move and trees to
      speak;
Augurs and understood relations have
125 By maggot-pies, and choughs, and rooks, brought
      forth
The secret'st man of blood. What is the night?

Lady Macbeth
Almost at odds with morning, which is which.

Macbeth
How sayst thou, that Macduff denies his person
At our great bidding?

Lady Macbeth   Did you send to him, sir?

Macbeth
130 I hear it by the way; but I will send.
There's not a one of them but in his house
I keep a servant fee'd. I will to-morrow—
And betimes I will—to the weird sisters:
More shall they speak; for now I am bent to know,
135 By the worst means, the worst. For mine own good
All causes shall give way: I am in blood
Stepp'd in so far, that, should I wade no more,
Returning were as tedious as go o'er.
Strange things I have in head that will to hand,
140 Which must be acted ere they may be scann'd.

---

116   *mine :* the redness of his cheeks.
       blanch'd : turned white.

119   Pay no attention to the formalities
       with which you should leave.

122   *blood . . . blood :* murder demands
       to be avenged with the death of the
       murderer.
123   *Stones . . . move :* i.e. to reveal a
       buried corpse.
124-6 Speaking birds (such as the
       magpie, jackdaw, and rook) have
       given omens and signs ('Augurs') that
       can be understood, to reveal the most
       secretive murderer.
126   *What is the night :* what time (of
       night) is it?
127   *at odds :* disputing with.
       which is which : whether it is night
       or morning.
128   *denies his person :* refuses to come
       himself.

131-2 I have a paid servant (a spy) in
       every man's house.
132   *will :* will go.
133   *betimes :* early.
134   *bent :* determined.
135   *By the worst means :* in the worst
       way.
135-6 Everything shall be sacrificed
       (made to 'give way') to what I want.
138   *tedious :* troublesome.
       as go o'er : as to cross to the other
       side.
139   *will to hand :* need to be done.
140   They must be performed before
       they are studied.

Lady Macbeth
You lack the season of all natures, sleep.
Macbeth
Come, we'll to sleep. My strange and self-abuse
Is the initiate fear that wants hard use:
We are yet but young in deed.   [*Exeunt*

Scene 5 *On the moor*

Thunder. Enter the three Witches,
meeting Hecate
First Witch
Why, how now, Hecate! you look angrily.
Hecate
Have I not reason, beldams as you are,
Saucy and overbold? How did you dare
To trade and traffic with Macbeth
5 In riddles and affairs of death;
And I, the mistress of your charms,
The close contriver of all harms,
Was never call'd to bear my part,
Or show the glory of our art?
10 And, which is worse, all you have done
Hath been but for a wayward son,
Spiteful and wrathful; who, as others do,
Loves for his own ends, not for you.
But make amends now: get you gone,
15 And at the pit of Acheron
Meet me i' the morning: thither he
Will come to know his destiny:
Your vessels and your spells provide,
Your charms and everything beside.
20 I am for the air; this night I'll spend
Unto a dismal and a fatal end:
Great business must be wrought ere noon:
Upon the corner of the moon
There hangs a vaporous drop profound;
25 I'll catch it ere it come to ground:
And that, distill'd by magic sleights,
Shall raise such artificial sprites
As by the strength of their illusion
Shall draw him on to his confusion:

141   *season :* preservative.

142-3 My strange self-deception is like the fear of a beginner ('initiate') who needs practice.
144   *young :* inexperienced.

Act 3   scene 5
The Witches meet again, and Hecate, their Queen, scolds them for speaking to Macbeth. She orders them to meet her at another time, when Macbeth will come to ask for more knowledge. This scene was probably not written by Shakespeare, but added to the play because the audience liked to see the witches.
2   *beldams :* old hags.
3   *Saucy :* impudent.
4   *traffic :* deal.

7   *close contriver :* secret planner.

9   *art :* i.e. witchcraft.

12-13 Macbeth does not love evil for its own sake, but only for what it can do for him.

15   *Acheron :* a river in the Greek underworld.

24   *vaporous drop profound.* It was believed that the moon shed a foam, with magical powers ('profound'), on to various herbs.
26   *sleights :* tricks.
27   *sprites :* spirits, ghosts.
29   *confusion :* damnation.

30-1 He will have high hopes, above the
      reach of wisdom.

32   *security* : over-confidence.

30 He shall spurn fate, scorn death, and bear
    His hopes 'bove wisdom, grace, and fear;
    And you all know, security
    Is mortals' chiefest enemy.
                              [*A song is sung offstage*
    Hark! I am call'd; my little spirit, see,
35 Sits in a foggy cloud, and stays for me.   [*Exit*
        First Witch
    Come, let's make haste; she'll soon be back again.
                                              [*Exeunt*

Act 3   scene 6

Lennox talks to another Lord, and
reminds him of what has happened.
We can tell from the irony of his words
that Lennox (and probably many
others) is now suspicious of Macbeth.
The Lord can give some information
about Duncan's son Malcolm, and
about Macduff.

1-2   I have only spoken what you are
      thinking, and your own thoughts can
      work out the meaning in full.

3   *borne* : managed.

4   *marry* : by [the Virgin] Mary; the
      oath was very commonly used, and is
      not strong.

8   *cannot . . . thought* : can fail to think.

10   *fact* : deed.

11   *straight* : immediately.

13   *thralls* : captives.

16   *deny 't* : deny that they had murdered
      Duncan.

17   *borne* : managed.

18   *under his key* : locked up.

19   *an't* : if.

21   *broad words* : gossip.

24   *bestows himself* : is staying.

Scene 6 *Forres. A room in the palace*

Enter Lennox *and another* Lord
    Lennox
My former speeches have but hit your thoughts,
Which can interpret further: only, I say,
Things have been strangely borne. The gracious
    Duncan
Was pitied of Macbeth: marry, he was dead:
5 And the right-valiant Banquo walk'd too late;
Whom, you may say, if 't please you, Fleance kill'd,
For Fleance fled: men must not walk too late.
Who cannot want the thought, how monstrous
It was for Malcolm and for Donalbain
10 To kill their gracious father? damned fact!
How it did grieve Macbeth! did he not straight
In pious rage the two delinquents tear,
That were the slaves of drink and thralls of sleep?
Was not that nobly done? Ay, and wisely too;
15 For 'twould have anger'd any heart alive
To hear the men deny 't. So that, I say,
He has borne all things well; and I do think
That, had he Duncan's sons under his key—
As, an't please heaven, he shall not—they should
    find
20 What 'twere to kill a father; so should Fleance.
But, peace! for from broad words, and 'cause he
    fail'd
His presence at the tyrant's feast, I hear
Macduff lives in disgrace. Sir, can you tell
Where he bestows himself?

25	*holds . . . birth :* witholds his birthright (i.e. the crown).
27	*Of :* by.
	Edward : Edward the Confessor, king of England 1042–66.
28–9	He does not lose any honour because of his misfortunes.
30	*upon his aid :* in support of Malcolm.
31	Siward, Earl of Northumberland, and Young Siward, his son.
33	*ratify :* sanction.
36	*free :* honest.
38	*exasperate :* angered.
40	*absolute :* curt.
	'Sir, not I'. This was Macduff's reply to Macbeth.
41	*cloudy :* sullen.
	turns me. The word 'me' here is used for emphasis only.
42	*hums :* murmurs.
43	*clogs :* burdens. The messenger would know that Macbeth was angry with messengers who brought bad news—see 5, 5, 38–40.
44	Warn him to be cautious and keep as far from Macbeth as his wisdom can take him.

Lord   The son of Duncan,

25 From whom this tyrant holds the due of birth,
  Lives in the English court, and is receiv'd
  Of the most pious Edward with such grace
  That the malevolence of fortune nothing
  Takes from his high respect. Thither Macduff
30 Is gone to pray the holy king, upon his aid
  To wake Northumberland and war-like Siward:
  That, by the help of these—with Him above
  To ratify the work—we may again
  Give to our tables meat, sleep to our nights,
35 Free from our feasts and banquets bloody knives,
  Do faithful homage and receive free honours;
  All which we pine for now. And this report
  Hath so exasperate the king that he
  Prepares for some attempt of war.

Lennox   Sent he to Macduff?

Lord

40 He did: and with an absolute, 'Sir, not I,'
  The cloudy messenger turns me his back,
  And hums, as who should say, 'You'll rue the time
  That clogs me with this answer.'

Lennox   And that well might

  Advise him to a caution to hold what distance
45 His wisdom can provide. Some holy angel
  Fly to the court of England and unfold
  His message ere he come, that a swift blessing
  May soon return to this our suffering country
  Under a hand accurs'd!

Lord   I'll send my prayers with him!

                                                    [*Exeunt*

Act 4

Act 4   scene 1

The witches gather on the moor to meet Macbeth. He makes them promise to answer his questions, and they conjure up magic apparitions which at first comfort, and then alarm him.

1   *brinded :* brindled (brown, with stripes of some other colour).

2   *hedge-pig :* hedgehog (a small wild animal with a snout like a pig's, covered with sharp prickles).

3   *Harpier :* the name of the witch's 'familiar' (see Introduction, p. xi), perhaps suggested to Shakespeare by the word 'harpy'—a monster, half-woman and half-bird, in Greek mythology.

8   *swelter'd :* sweated.
     venom : poison. All the ingredients of the witches' cooking-pot were thought by the Elizabethans to be poisonous, or at least unnatural.
     sleeping got : caught while it was asleep.

12   *Fillet :* slice.
     fenny : from the fens (low-lying, marshy land).

15   *Wool of bat :* the short hair nearest the skin of a bat (which is a smooth-haired animal).

16   *fork :* forked tongue.
     blind-worm : slow-worm (a kind of legless lizard).

17   *howlet :* owlet (a baby owl).

19   *hell-broth :* a thick soup, strong enough for the devil.

23   *mummy :* a medicine, either powder or liquid, made by witches and also by reputable doctors, from dead bodies.
     maw and gulf : stomach and throat.

Scene 1 *A cave on the moor. In the centre is a boiling cauldron*

Thunder. Enter the three Witches
First Witch
Thrice the brinded cat hath mew'd.
Second Witch
Thrice and once the hedge-pig whin'd.
Third Witch
Harpier cries: 'Tis time, 'tis time.
First Witch
Round about the cauldron go;
5   In the poison'd entrails throw.
Toad, that under cold stone
Days and nights hast thirty-one
Swelter'd venom, sleeping got,
Boil thou first i' the charmed pot.
All
10 Double, double, toil and trouble;
Fire burn and cauldron bubble.
Second Witch
Fillet of a fenny snake,
In the cauldron boil and bake;
Eye of newt, and toe of frog,
15 Wool of bat, and tongue of dog,
Adder's fork, and blind-worm's sting,
Lizard's leg, and howlet's wing,
For a charm of powerful trouble,
Like a hell-broth boil and bubble.
All
20 Double, double, toil and trouble;
Fire burn and cauldron bubble.
Third Witch
Scale of dragon, tooth of wolf,
Witches' mummy, maw and gulf

24   *ravin'd :* glutted (so its stomach
   would be full of human flesh).

25   *i' the dark.* Night was the best
   time for gathering poisonous herbs and
   roots.

27   *slips :* cuttings.

28   *Sliver'd :* sliced off.

31   *Ditch-deliver'd :* born in a ditch.
   drab : whore.

32   *slab :* sticky.

33   *chaudron :* entrails.

39–43   These lines, like the whole of
   Act 3, scene 5, were probably not
   written by Shakespeare.

39   I am pleased by the trouble that
   you have taken.

50   I call upon you, in the name of
   the magic that you practice.

51   *Howe'er . . . it :* i.e. even if you
   have learned it from the devil.

53   *yesty :* yeasty (because they foam,
   like a liquid to which yeast has been
   added).

25   Of the ravin'd salt-sea shark,
   Root of hemlock digg'd i' the dark,
   Liver of blaspheming Jew,
   Gall of goat, and slips of yew
   Sliver'd in the moon's eclipse,
   Nose of Turk, and Tartar's lips,
30   Finger of birth-strangled babe
   Ditch-deliver'd by a drab,
   Make the gruel thick and slab;
   Add thereto a tiger's cauldron,
   For the ingredients of our cauldron.
        All
35   Double, double, toil and trouble;
   Fire burn and cauldron bubble.
        Second Witch
   Cool it with a baboon's blood,
   Then the charm is firm and good.

        Enter Hecate
        Hecate
   O well done! I commend your pains,
40   And every one shall share i' the gains.
   And now about the cauldron sing,
   Like elves and fairies in a ring,
   Enchanting all that you put in.
                              [*They sing*

        Second Witch
   By the pricking of my thumbs,
45   Something wicked this way comes.
        Open, locks,
        Whoever knocks.

        Enter Macbeth
        Macbeth
   How now, you secret, black, and midnight hags!
   What is 't you do?
        All   A deed without a name.
        Macbeth
50   I conjure you, by that which you profess—
   Howe'er you come to know it—answer me:
   Though you untie the winds and let them fight
   Against the churches; though the yesty waves

54   *Confound* : confuse.
      navigation : shipping.
55   *bladed* : unripe (the corn is still a
      'blade', not yet an 'ear').
      lodg'd : blown flat.
57   *slope* : bend.

59   *Nature's germens* : the seeds of all
      creation.
60   *till destruction sicken* : until
      destruction itself is sick (because so
      much has been destroyed).

63   *our masters* : i.e. the evil spirits they
      serve.

65   *nine farrow* : litter of nine piglets
      (only an unnatural sow would do this,
      and therefore her blood would be
      poisonous).
      sweaten : sweated.
68   *office* : function.

68sd *Apparition.* The Apparitions rose
      through a trapdoor in the stage, and
      then 'descended' again.

73   *caution* : advice.
74   *harp'd* : guessed.
      aright : correctly.

Confound and swallow navigation up;
55 Though bladed corn be lodg'd, and trees blown
      down;
Though castles topple on their warders' heads;
Though palaces and pyramids do slope
Their heads to their foundations; though the
      treasure
Of Nature's germens tumble all together,
60 Even till destruction sicken—answer me
To what I ask you.
              First Witch   Speak.
              Second Witch   Demand.
              Third Witch   We'll answer.
              First Witch
Say if thou'dst rather hear it from our mouths,
Or from our masters'?
              Macbeth   Call 'em: let me see 'em.
              First Witch
Pour in sow's blood, that hath eaten
65 Her nine farrow; grease that's sweaten
From the murderer's gibbet, throw
Into the flame.
              All   Come, high or low;
Thyself and office deftly show.

              Thunder. First Apparition : *an armed Head*
              Macbeth
Tell me, thou unknown power,—
              First Witch   He knows thy thought :
70 Hear his speech, but say thou nought.
              First Apparition
Macbeth! Macbeth! Macbeth! beware Macduff;
Beware the Thane of Fife. Dismiss me. Enough.
                                        [*Descends*
              Macbeth
Whate'er thou art, for thy good caution thanks;
Thou hast harp'd my fear aright. But one word
      more—
              First Witch
75 He will not be commanded: here's another,

More potent than the first.

Thunder. Second Apparition : *a bloody Child*

Second Apparition
Macbeth! Macbeth! Macbeth!—
Macbeth
Had I three ears, I'd hear thee.
Second Apparition
Be bloody, bold, and resolute; laugh to scorn
80 The power of man, for none of woman born
Shall harm Macbeth.   [*Descends*
Macbeth
Then live, Macduff: what need I fear of thee?
But yet I'll make assurance double sure,
And take a bond of fate: thou shalt not live;
85 That I may tell pale-hearted fear it lies,
And sleep in spite of thunder.

Thunder. Third Apparition : *a Child crowned, with a tree in his hand*
                              What is this,
That rises like the issue of a king,
And wears upon his baby brow the round
And top of sovereignty?
All   Listen, but speak not to 't.
Third Apparition
90 Be lion-mettl'd, proud, and take no care
Who chafes, who frets, or where conspirers are:
Macbeth shall never vanquish'd be until
Great Birnam Wood to high Dunsinane Hill
Shall come against him.   [*Descends*
Macbeth   That will never be:
95 Who can impress the forest, bid the tree
Unfix his earth-bound root? Sweet bodements!
    good!
Rebellious dead, rise never till the wood
Of Birnam rise, and our high-plac'd Macbeth
Shall live the lease of nature, pay his breath
100 To time and mortal custom. Yet my heart
Throbs to know one thing: tell me—if your art
Can tell so much—shall Banquo's issue ever
Reign in this kingdom?

83-4   I will make doubly sure, and guarantee ('take a bond') that fate keeps its word.
84   *thou :* i.e. Macduff.
85   So that I may tell my fears that they are false.
86   *thunder.* Thunder was often thought to be the voice of God, reminding the evil-doer of his crimes, and warning him to repent.
87   *issue :* offspring.
88-9   *round And top :* i.e. the crown.

90   *lion-mettl'd :* lion-hearted.
91   *chafes :* is angry.
    frets : complains.
93   Birnam Wood was about twelve miles from Dunsinane.

95   *impress :* enlist (as a soldier).
96   *bodements :* prophecies.

99   *the lease of nature :* have a natural lease (or length) of life.
99-100   Give up his breath (as if he were paying a debt) to old age and the natural causes of death.
101   *Throbs :* desires.

111sd   *show :* dumb-show.

glass. This might be either a
mirror, held in such a way that it
reflected several more kings behind the
eighth, or else some kind of magic
'crystal ball'.

112-24   The eight kings pass, one at
a time, in front of Macbeth, and he
comments on each one as it passes
him.

113   *sear :* burn.

hair : appearance.

116   *Start, eyes :* let my eyeballs fall
from their sockets.

117   *crack of doom :* the dawning of
Doomsday.

121   The double orb refers to the
coronation of King James at both
Scone (as James VI of Scotland) and
Westminster (as James I of England);
a single sceptre is used in the Scottish
ceremony, and two in the English
coronation. See Introduction, p. vii.
See illustration, p. 65.

123   *blood-bolter'd :* hair clotted with
blood.

All   Seek to know no more.

Macbeth

I will be satisfied: deny me this,

105   And an eternal curse fall on you! Let me know.

Why sinks that cauldron? and what noise is this?

[Music; the cauldron descends

First Witch

Show!

Second Witch

Show!

Third Witch

Show!

All

110   Show his eyes, and grieve his heart;

Come like shadows, so depart.

A show of Eight Kings; the last with a glass
in his hand : Banquo *following*

Macbeth

Thou art too like the spirit of Banquo; down!

Thy crown does sear mine eyeballs: and thy hair,

Thou other gold-bound brow, is like the first:

115   A third is like the former. Filthy hags!

Why do you show me this? A fourth! Start, eyes!

What! will the line stretch out to the crack of doom?

Another yet? A seventh! I'll see no more:

And yet the eighth appears, who bears a glass

120   Which shows me many more; and some I see

That two-fold balls and treble sceptres carry.

Horrible sight! Now, I see, 'tis true;

For the blood-bolter'd Banquo smiles upon me,

And points at them for his.   *[Apparitions vanish*

What! is this so?

First Witch

125   Ay, sir, all this is so: but why

Stands Macbeth thus amazedly?

Come sisters, cheer we up his sprites,

And show the best of our delights.

I'll charm the air to give a sound,

130   While you perform your antick round,

That this great king may kindly say

Our duties did his welcome pay.

127   *sprites* : spirits.
130   *antick round* : comic dance (in a circle around Macbeth).
132   Our homage has paid him the welcome due to him.
134   *aye* : for ever.
135   *without there* : whoever is outside (offstage).

[*Music. The Witches dance, and then vanish with* Hecate

Macbeth
Where are they? Gone? Let this pernicious hour
Stand aye accursed in the calendar!
135 Come in, without there!

Enter Lennox

Lennox   What's your Grace's will?
Macbeth
Saw you the weird sisters?
Lennox   No, my lord.
Macbeth
Came they not by you?
Lennox   No indeed, my lord.
Macbeth
Infected be the air whereon they ride,
And damn'd all those that trust them! I did hear
140 The galloping of horse: who was 't came by?
Lennox
'Tis two or three, my lord, that bring you word
Macduff is fled to England.
Macbeth   Fled to England!
Lennox
Ay, my good lord.
Macbeth
[*Aside*] Time, thou anticipat'st my dread exploits;

145-6   You can never be as fast as you intend to be unless you perform a deed as soon as you think of it.
147-8   The first conceptions of my heart shall be the first acts of my hand.
149   *crown* : complete.

151   *Fife* : i.e. Macduff.

153   *trace . . . line* : descend from him, are of his lineage.

155   *sights* : the apparitions.

145 The flighty purpose never is o'ertook
Unless the deed go with it; from this moment
The very firstlings of my heart shall be
The firstlings of my hand. And even now,
To crown my thoughts with acts, be it thought and done:
150 The castle of Macduff I will surprise;
Seize upon Fife; give to the edge of the sword
His wife, his babes, and all unfortunate souls
That trace him in his line. No boasting like a fool;
This deed I'll do before this purpose cool:
155 But no more sights! [*Aloud*] Where are these gentlemen?
Come, bring me where they are.   [*Exeunt*

Act 4   scene 2

Lady Macduff questions Ross about her husband's flight, and then tries to explain the situation to her little son. A Messenger warns her to flee from the palace, but it is too late. The murderers rush into the room.

3-4   When we are not traitors for what we have done, we are still traitors by being afraid and running away.

7   *titles* : possessions, things he is entitled to.

9   *wants* : lacks.
       natural touch : instincts.

12-15 When it is so unreasonable to run away, it shows neither love (for his family) nor wisdom, but only fear (for himself).

14   *coz* : cousin (but they are probably not related).

15   *school* : control.
       for : as for.

16   *judicious* : of good judgement.

17   *fits o' the season* : moods of the times.

18-19 *we are . . . ourselves* : we are false to those things we say we believe in, and we do not understand our own actions.

19-20 Fears make us believe rumours.

22   *Each . . . move* : move backwards and forwards.

23   *Shall* : it will.
       but : before.

24   *climb upward* : improve.

Scene 2 *Fife. A room in Macduff's castle*

Enter Lady Macduff, *her* Son, *and* Ross

Lady Macduff
What had he done to make him fly the land?
   Ross
You must have patience, madam.
   Lady Macduff   He had none:
His flight was madness: when our actions do not,
Our fears do make us traitors.
   Ross   You know not
5 Whether it was his wisdom or his fear.
   Lady Macduff
Wisdom! to leave his wife, to leave his babes,
His mansion and his titles in a place
From whence himself does fly? He loves us not;
He wants the natural touch; for the poor wren,
10 The most diminutive of birds, will fight—
Her young ones in her nest—against the owl.
All is the fear and nothing is the love;
As little is the wisdom, where the flight
So runs against all reason.
   Ross   My dearest coz,
15 I pray you, school yourself: but, for your husband,
He is noble, wise, judicious, and best knows
The fits o' the season. I dare not speak much further:
But cruel are the times, when we are traitors
And do not know ourselves; when we hold rumour
20 From what we fear, yet know not what we fear,
But float upon a wild and violent sea
Each way, and move. I take my leave of you:
Shall not be long but I'll be here again.
Things at the worst will cease, or else climb upward
25 To what they were before. My pretty cousin,
Blessing upon you!

Lady Macduff
Father'd he is, and yet he's fatherless.
   Ross
I am so much a fool, should I stay longer,
It would be my disgrace, and your discomfort:
30 I take my leave at once.   [*Exit*
      Lady Macduff   Sirrah, your father's dead:
And what will you do now? How will you live?
      Son
As birds do, mother.
      Lady Macduff   What! with worms and flies?
      Son
With what I get, I mean; and so do they.
      Lady Macduff
Poor bird! thou'dst never fear the net nor lime,
35 The pit-fall nor the gin?
      Son
Why should I, mother? Poor birds they are not
   set for.
My father is not dead, for all your saying.
      Lady Macduff
Yes, he is dead: how wilt thou do for a father?
      Son
Nay, how will you do for a husband?
      Lady Macduff
40 Why, I can buy me twenty at any market.
      Son
Then you'll buy 'em to sell again.
      Lady Macduff
Thou speak'st with all thy wit; and yet, i' faith,
With wit enough for thee.
      Son
Was my father a traitor, mother?
      Lady Macduff
45 Ay, that he was.
      Son
What is a traitor?
      Lady Macduff
Why, one that swears and lies.

28-9   If Ross were to stay, he would be
   so foolish as to weep; this would be
   a disgrace to him, and an embarrass-
   ment to Lady Macduff.
30   *Sirrah*. A term of endearment (as
   used here), or abuse.

34   *lime*. The birds' feet stuck in the
   lime, and they were caught.
35   *pit-fall*: snare.
   gin: trap.
36   *Poor . . . for*: they are not set to
   catch poor birds (only those with rich
   plumage).

41   If you can get them so easily, you
   will not want to keep them.
42   *wit*: intelligence.
43   *for thee*: for your age.

Son
And be all traitors that do so?

Lady Macduff
Every one that does so is a traitor, and must be
hanged.

Son
50 And must they all be hanged that swear and lie?

Lady Macduff
Every one.

Son
Who must hang them?

Lady Macduff
Why, the honest men.

Son
Then the liars and swearers are fools, for there are
55 liars and swearers enow to beat the honest men,
and hang up them.

Lady Macduff
Now God help thee, poor monkey! But how wilt
thou do for a father?

Son
If he were dead, you'd weep for him: if you would
60 not, it were a good sign that I should quickly have
a new father.

Lady Macduff
Poor prattler, how thou talk'st!

Enter a Messenger

Messenger
Bless you, fair dame! I am not to you known,
Though in your state of honour I am perfect.
65 I doubt some danger does approach you nearly:
If you will take a homely man's advice,
Be not found here; hence, with your little ones.
To fright you thus, methinks, I am too savage;
To do worse to you were fell cruelty,
70 Which is too nigh your person. Heaven preserve
you!
I dare abide no longer.   [*Exit*

Lady Macduff   Whither should I fly?
I have done no harm. But I remember now,
I am in this earthly world, where to do harm
Is often laudable, to do good sometime

55   *enow :* enough.

59–60   *would not :* would not weep.

62   *prattler :* chatterbox.

64   I know your rank very well.

65   *doubt :* suspect.
       nearly : closely.

66   *homely :* humble.

68   *savage :* cruel.

69   *fell :* pitiless.

70   Which is already too close to you.

75 Accounted dangerous folly; why then, alas!
Do I put up that womanly defence,
To say I have done no harm?

Enter Murderers

What are these faces?

Murderer
Where is your husband?

Lady Macduff
I hope in no place so unsanctified
80 Where such as thou mayst find him.

Murderer   He's a traitor.

Son
Thou liest, thou shag-hair'd villain.

Murderer   What, you egg!
Young fry of treachery!   [*Stabbing him*

Son   He has kill'd me, mother:
Run away, I pray you!   [*Dies*
          [*Exit* Lady Macduff, *crying 'Murder', and
                    pursued by the* Murderers

Scene 3 *England. Outside the king's palace*

Enter Malcolm *and* Macduff

Malcolm
Let us seek out some desolate shade, and there
Weep our sad bosoms empty.

Macduff   Let us rather
Hold fast the mortal sword, and like good men
Bestride our down-fall'n birthdom. Each new morn
5 New widows howl, new orphans cry, new sorrows
Strike heaven on the face, that it resounds
As if it felt with Scotland, and yell'd out
Like syllable of dolour.

Malcolm   What I believe I'll wail,
What know, believe; and what I can redress,

---

81   *shag-hair'd :* with shaggy hair.

82   *fry :* spawn, young fish.

Act 4   scene 3
Safely away from Scotland, Macduff
has been telling Malcolm about the
sufferings of his country. At first
Malcolm does not trust Macduff. He
tells him that he (Malcolm) will be a
greater tyrant than Macbeth, because
he has more vices. Macduff is
distressed, but when Malcolm sees
the sorrow he explains that he told lies
about himself to test Macduff's
loyalty. We hear about the holy
English king, whose touch cures
sickness. Ross brings bad news to
Macduff.

2   *bosoms :* hearts.
3   *mortal :* deadly.
4   *Bestride :* defend.
      birthdom : country of our birth.
6-8   The grief cries up to heaven, and
      the skies seem to feel Scotland's
      sorrow, for heaven's cries echo the
      same note.
8   *Like :* the same.
8-10   I will lament for what I believe,
      believe only what I know to be true,
      and do what I can to put things right
      when the time is favourable ('to
      friend').

11   Perhaps what you say is true.

12   *whose sole name :* whose name alone.

14   *touch'd :* harmed.

14-15 *I am . . . me :* although I am only young, you may gain something from him by betraying me.

15   *wisdom :* it is good sense.

16   *lamb :* Malcolm means himself.

19   *recoil :* turn away from virtue.

20   *In . . . charge :* at a royal command.
      crave : beg.

21   My thoughts cannot change your nature.

22   Although Lucifer, the 'brightest' angel, fell from God's grace, we must not assume that all angels are like him; some are pure and 'bright' still.

23-4 Although evil tries to look virtuous, virtue is no less virtuous than it ever was.

5   *Perchance :* perhaps.
      even there. Macduff was hoping that he could help to overthrow Macbeth, but in his flight to England he lost his hopes. But the suddenness of this flight has aroused Malcolm's suspicions.

26   *rawness :* exposure to danger.

27   *motives :* incentives.
      knots of love : ties of affection.

28   *leave-taking :* saying 'goodbye'.

29-30 Do not think my suspicions do you any dishonour; they are to protect me.

30   *rightly just :* truly honest.

32-4 Tyranny may lay its foundations securely, since righteousness (in the person of Malcolm) dare not stop it. Macbeth can wear his stolen crown, for his title is confirmed ('affeered' is a legal term) by Malcolm's weakness.

37   *to boot :* in addition.

38   I do not speak like this just because I am afraid of you.

39   *yoke :* i.e. the rule of Macbeth. The 'yoke' fastens oxen to the plough they are pulling.

41   *withal :* as well.

10 As I shall find the time to friend, I will.
    What you have spoke, it may be so, perchance.
    This tyrant, whose sole name blisters our tongues,
    Was once thought honest; you have lov'd him well;
    He hath not touch'd you yet. I am young, but something
15 You may deserve of him through me, and wisdom
    To offer up a weak, poor, innocent lamb
    T' appease an angry god.
        Macduff
    I am not treacherous.
        Malcolm   But Macbeth is.
    A good and virtuous nature may recoil
20 In an imperial charge. But I shall crave your pardon;
    That which you are my thoughts cannot transpose;
    Angels are bright still, though the brightest fell;
    Though all things foul would wear the brows of grace,
    Yet grace must still look so.
        Macduff   I have lost my hopes.
        Malcolm
25 Perchance even there where I did find my doubts.
    Why in that rawness left you wife and child—
    Those precious motives, those strong knots of love—
    Without leave-taking? I pray you,
    Let not my jealousies be your dishonours,
30 But mine own safeties: you may be rightly just,
    Whatever I shall think.
        Macduff   Bleed, bleed, poor country!
    Great tyranny, lay thou thy basis sure,
    For goodness dare not check thee! wear thou thy wrongs;
    The title is affeer'd! Fare thee well, lord:
35 I would not be the villain that thou think'st
    For the whole space that's in the tyrant's grasp,
    And the rich East to boot.
        Malcolm   Be not offended:
    I speak not as in absolute fear of you.
    I think our country sinks beneath the yoke;
40 It weeps, it bleeds, and each new day a gash
    Is added to her wounds: I think withal

43   *gracious England :* i.e. Edward the
Confessor.
44   *goodly thousands :* thousands of good
soldiers.
46   *wear :* carry.

48-9   Shall suffer more, and suffer in
more different ways, than ever before.

51   *particulars of vice :* individual vices.
grafted : implanted.
52   *open'd :* developed (they have been
planted like flowers, and will open as
buds open).
55   *confineless harms :* boundless evils.

57   *top :* surpass.

58   *Luxurious :* lustful.
59   *Sudden :* violent.
smacking : tasting.
61   *voluptuousness :* lechery.

63   *cistern :* tank (as a water-tank).
63-5   My lust would break down all the
obstacles that chastity ('continence')
set up against my will.
66   *such an one :* a man like this.
66-7   Complete lack of self-control is
a tyranny in man's nature.
67-9   It has caused many thrones to
become vacant before the proper time.

71   *Convey :* secretly conduct.
in a spacious plenty : where there is
plenty of room.
72   *cold :* chaste.
the time : the age (or 'the people').
hoodwink : deceive.
73-6   Who will offer themselves (as
mistresses) to the king, as soon as they
know what his desires are.

There would be hands uplifted in my right;
And here from gracious England have I offer
Of goodly thousands. But, for all this,
45 When I shall tread upon the tyrant's head,
Or wear it on my sword, yet my poor country
Shall have more vices than it had before,
More suffer, and more sundry ways than ever,
By him that shall succeed.
    Macduff   What should he be?
    Malcolm
50 It is myself I mean; in whom I know
All the particulars of vice so grafted,
That, when they shall be open'd, black Macbeth
Will seem as pure as snow, and the poor state
Esteem him as a lamb, being compar'd
55 With my confineless harms.
    Macduff   Not in the legions
Of horrid hell can come a devil more damn'd
In evils to top Macbeth.
    Malcolm   I grant him bloody,
Luxurious, avaricious, false, deceitful,
Sudden, malicious, smacking of every sin
60 That has a name; but there's no bottom, none,
In my voluptuousness: your wives, your daughters,
Your matrons, and your maids, could not fill up
The cistern of my lust, and my desire
All continent impediments would o'erbear
65 That did oppose my will; better Macbeth
Than such an one to reign.
    Macduff   Boundless intemperance
In nature is a tyranny; it hath been
Th' untimely emptying of the happy throne,
And fall of many kings. But fear not yet
70 To take upon you what is yours; you may
Convey your pleasures in a spacious plenty,
And yet seem cold—the time you may so hoodwink.
We have willing dames enough; there cannot be
That vulture in you, to devour so many

75 As will to greatness dedicate themselves,
Finding it so inclin'd.
    Malcolm   With this there grows
In my most ill-compos'd affection such
A staunchless avarice that, were I king,
I should cut off the nobles for their lands,
80 Desire his jewels and this other's house;
And my more-having would be as a sauce
To make me hunger more, that I should forge
Quarrels unjust against the good and loyal,
Destroying them for wealth.
    Macduff   This avarice
85 Sticks deeper, grows with more pernicious root
Than summer-seeming lust; and it hath been
The sword of our slain kings: yet do not fear;
Scotland hath foisons to fill up your will,
Of your mere own; all these are portable
90 With other graces weigh'd.
    Malcolm
But I have none: the king-becoming graces,
As justice, verity, temperance, stableness,
Bounty, perseverance, mercy, lowliness,
Devotion, patience, courage, fortitude—
95 I have no relish of them, but abound
In the division of each several crime,
Acting it many ways. Nay, had I power, I should
Pour the sweet milk of concord into hell,
Uproar the universal peace, confound
100 All unity on earth.
    Macduff   O Scotland, Scotland!
    Malcolm
If such a one be fit to govern, speak;
I am as I have spoken.
    Macduff   Fit to govern!
No, not to live. O nation miserable,
With an untitled tyrant bloody-scepter'd!
105 When shalt thou see thy wholesome days again,
Since that the truest issue of thy throne
By his own interdiction stands accus'd,

---

77   *ill-compos'd affection :* unbalanced nature.

78   *staunchless :* unsatisfied.

79   *cut off :* kill.

80   *his . . . house :* this man's jewels, and that man's house.

81   *my more-having :* the more I had.

85   *sticks deeper :* is a more deeply-rooted vice.

86   *summer-seeming lust :* lust is only fit for the summer of man's life, and dies away with the winter of age.

87   *The sword :* the cause of death.

88-9 Scotland has rich harvests ('foisons') of wealth that will satisfy you, merely from your own estates.

89   *portable :* bearable.

90   Balanced against your virtues.

91   *king-becoming graces :* virtues appropriate to a king.

92   *verity :* truth.
      stableness : constancy.

93   *Bounty :* generosity.
      lowliness : humility.

95   *no relish :* no trace.

96   *division :* variations.
      several : separate.

97-8 If I could, I would say 'To hell with harmony'.

99   *Uproar :* cause uproar in.
      confound : destroy.

104   *untitled :* without hereditary right to the throne.
      bloody-scepter'd : Macbeth has obtained the throne through bloodshed, and it is as though his sceptre were stained with blood.

105   *wholesome :* good, healthy.

106   *truest issue :* true heir.

107-8 By banning himself from Scotland, he is convicted ('stands accus'd') of evil, and slanders his family.

Edward the Confessor

And does blaspheme his breed? Thy royal father
Was a most sainted king; the queen that bore thee,
110 Oft'ner upon her knees than on her feet,
Died every day she liv'd. Fare thee well!
These evils thou repeat'st upon thyself
Have banish'd me from Scotland. O my breast,
Thy hope ends here!
  Malcolm   Macduff, this noble passion,
115 Child of integrity, hath from my soul
Wip'd the black scruples, reconcil'd my thoughts
To thy good truth and honour. Devilish Macbeth
By many of these trains hath sought to win me
Into his power, and modest wisdom plucks me
120 From over-credulous haste; but God above
Deal between thee and me! for even now
I put myself to thy direction, and
Unspeak mine own detraction, here abjure
The taints and blames I laid upon myself,
125 For strangers to my nature. I am yet
Unknown to woman; never was forsworn;
Scarcely have coveted what was mine own;
At no time broke my faith; would not betray
The devil to his fellow; and delight
130 No less in truth than life; my first false speaking
Was this upon myself. What I am truly,
Is thine and my poor country's to command;
Whither indeed, before thy here-approach,
Old Siward, with ten thousand warlike men,
135 Already at a point, was setting forth.
Now we'll together, and the chance of goodness
Be like our warranted quarrel. Why are you silent?
  Macduff
Such welcome and unwelcome things at once
'Tis hard to reconcile.

   Enter a Doctor
  Malcolm   Well, more anon.
140 Comes the king forth, I pray you?
  Doctor
Ay, sir; there are a crew of wretched souls
That stay his cure; their malady convinces

---

110 *upon her knees:* i.e. in prayer.

111 In her prayers, she made a daily
vow of rejecting ('dying to') sin.

112 *repeat'st . . . thyself:* accuse
yourself of.

113 *breast:* heart.

115 *Child of integrity.* Macduff's
grief for Scotland could only spring
from honesty.

116 *scruples:* suspicions.
  reconcil'd my thoughts: made me
trust you again.

118 *trains:* schemes.

119 *modest:* cautious.

119-20 Prevents me from trusting people
too quickly.

120-1 *but . . . me:* but now may God
direct the dealings between you and
me.

122 *to:* under.

123 I withdraw the accusations I
made against myself.
  abjure: renounce.

125 *For strangers:* as foreign.

126 *Unknown to woman:* a virgin.
  was forsworn: committed perjury.

133 *here-approach:* coming here.

135 *at a point:* ready.

136 *we'll together:* we'll go together.

136-7 May our chances of success
('goodness' = good fortune) be the
same as the justice (warranty) of the
cause ('quarrel') we fight for.

139 *more anon:* we'll talk more about
that later (the entry of the Doctor stops
their conversation).

142 *stay:* await.
  convinces: defeats.

143   *great assay of art :* greatest efforts of medical skill.

145   *presently amend :* recover at once.

146   *the Evil.* The 'King's Evil' was scrofula, a form of tuberculosis. It was thought that the king had a heavenly gift for healing this disease, and it was also believed (see lines 155-6) that this power was hereditary.

148   *here-remain :* staying here.

149   *solicits heaven :* prays to God for this power.

150   *visited :* afflicted.

152   *mere :* complete.

153   *a golden stamp :* a special medal, stamped with the figure of St. Michael; monarchs before King James made the sign of the cross over the patient with this medal, but James simply hung it round their necks.

154   *'tis spoken :* it is said.

156   *healing benediction :* blessed gift of healing.
       virtue : power.

158   *sundry :* various.

160   Ross's clothes would indicate that he was Scottish.

161   *ever-gentle :* always noble.
       cousin : kinsman.

162   *betimes :* quickly.

163   *means :* circumstances.

164   Is Scotland still the same as it was?

165   *Almost . . . itself :* the people of Scotland are almost afraid to know each other.

166-7 No-one is ever seen to smile, except those who do not know what is going on.

The great assay of art; but, at his touch,
Such sanctity hath heaven given his hand,
145 They presently amend.

Malcolm   I thank you, doctor.
                                                   [*Exit* Doctor

Macduff
What's the disease he means?

Malcolm   'Tis call'd the Evil:
A most miraculous work in this good king,
Which often, since my here-remain in England,
I have seen him do. How he solicits heaven,
150 Himself best knows; but strangely-visited people,
All swoln and ulcerous, pitiful to the eye,
The mere despair of surgery, he cures,
Hanging a golden stamp about their necks,
Put on with holy prayers; and 'tis spoken,
155 To the succeeding royalty he leaves
The healing benediction. With this strange virtue,
He hath a heavenly gift of prophecy,
And sundry blessings hang about his throne,
That speak him full of grace.

                    Enter Ross

Macduff   See, who comes here?

Malcolm
160 My countryman; but yet I know him not.

Macduff
My ever-gentle cousin, welcome hither.

Malcolm
I know him now. Good God, betimes remove
The means that makes us strangers!

Ross   Sir, amen.

Macduff
Stands Scotland where it did?

Ross   Alas! poor country;

165 Almost afraid to know itself. It cannot
Be call'd our mother, but our grave; where nothing,
But who knows nothing, is once seen to smile;

169   *not mark'd* : unnoticed.

170   *A modern ecstasy* : a commonplace emotion.

170-1 Hardly anyone bothers to ask who is dead when they hear a funeral bell ('knell').

173   *or ere* : before.
       relation : tale.

174   *nice* : accurate.
       newest : latest.

175   A sad story that is one hour old causes the teller to be hissed at (because it is out of date).

176   *teems* : is stocked with.
       does : is.

180   *niggard* : miser.

182   *heavily* : sadly.

183   *out* : out in the field (fighting against Macbeth).

184   The rumour was the more confirmed in my belief.

185   *For that* : because.
       power : forces.
       a-foot : on the march.

186   *of* : to.
       eye : appearance (he speaks to Malcolm).

188   *doff* : cast off (like clothes).
       Be 't their comfort : may it be a comfort to them.

189   *Gracious England* : i.e. Edward the Confessor.

191   *older* : more experienced.

191-2 *none . . . out* : no soldier in Christendom is said to be.

Where sighs and groans and shrieks that rent the air
Are made, not mark'd; where violent sorrow seems
170 A modern ecstasy; the dead man's knell
Is there scarce ask'd for who; and good men's lives
Expire before the flowers in their caps,
Dying or ere they sicken.
    Macduff   O relation
Too nice, and yet too true!
    Malcolm   What's the newest grief?
    Ross
175 That of an hour's age doth hiss the speaker;
Each minute teems a new one.
    Macduff   How does my wife?
    Ross '
Why, well.
    Macduff   And all my children?
    Ross   Well too.
    Macduff
The tyrant has not batter'd at their peace?
    Ross
No; they were well at peace when I did leave 'em.
    Macduff
180 Be not a niggard of your speech: how goes 't?
    Ross
When I came hither to transport the tidings,
Which I have heavily borne, there ran a rumour
Of many worthy fellows that were out;
Which was to my belief witness'd the rather
185 For that I saw the tyrant's power a-foot.
Now is the time of help; your eye in Scotland
Would create soldiers, make our women fight,
To doff their dire distresses.
    Malcolm   Be 't their comfort
We are coming thither. Gracious England hath
190 Lent us good Siward and ten thousand men—
An older and a better soldier none
That Christendom gives out.

193 *the like* : the same.
194 *would be* : ought to be.
195 *latch* : catch.

196 *a fee-grief* : a private grief.
197 *Due to* : owing to.

199 *Pertains* : belongs.

205 *the manner* : the way they were killed.
206 *quarry* : animals killed in a hunt.
    deer. There is a pun with 'dear'.

208 Macduff hides his face in his hat.

210 *Whispers* : whispers to.
    o'er-fraught : overloaded.

212 And I had to be away from there!

Ross   Would I could answer
This comfort with the like! But I have words
That would be howl'd out in the desert air,
195 Where hearing should not latch them.
    Macduff   What concern they?
The general cause? or is it a fee-grief
Due to some single breast?
    Ross   No mind that's honest
But in it shares some woe, though the main part
Pertains to you alone.
    Macduff   If it be mine
200 Keep it not from me; quickly let me have it.
    Ross
Let not your ears despise my tongue for ever,
Which shall possess them with the heaviest sound
That ever yet they heard.
    Macduff   Hum! I guess at it.
    Ross
Your castle is surpris'd; your wife and babes
205 Savagely slaughter'd; to relate the manner
Were, on the quarry of these murder'd deer,
To add the death of you.
    Malcolm   Merciful heaven!
What, man! ne'er pull your hat upon your brows;
Give sorrow words; the grief that does not speak
210 Whispers the o'er-fraught heart and bids it break.
    Macduff
My children too?
    Ross   Wife, children, servants, all
That could be found.
    Macduff   And I must be from thence!
My wife kill'd too?
    Ross   I have said.

Malcolm   Be comforted:
Let's make us medicine of our great revenge,
215 To cure this deadly grief.
     Macduff
He has no children. All my pretty ones?
Did you say all? O hell-kite! All?
What, all my pretty chickens and their dam
At one fell swoop?
     Malcolm   Dispute it like a man.
     Macduff
220 I shall do so;
But I must also feel it as a man:
I cannot but remember such things were,
That were most precious to me. Did heaven look on,
And would not take their part? Sinful Macduff!
225 They were all struck for thee. Naught that I am,
Not for their own demerits, but for mine,
Fell slaughter on their souls. Heaven rest them
    now.
     Malcolm
Be this the whetstone of your sword: let grief
Convert to anger; blunt not the heart, enrage it.
     Macduff
230 O, I could play the woman with mine eyes,
And braggart with my tongue. But, gentle heavens,
Cut short all intermission; front to front
Bring thou this fiend of Scotland and myself;
Within my sword's length set him; if he 'scape,
235 Heaven forgive him too!
     Malcolm   This tune goes manly.
Come, go we to the king; our power is ready;
Our lack is nothing but our leave. Macbeth
Is ripe for shaking, and the powers above
Put on their instruments. Receive what cheer you
    may;
240 The night is long that never finds the day.
                                              [*Exeunt*

---

216   *He . . . children.* This may refer
       to Malcolm (he would not speak so
       unfeelingly if he were a father); or it
       might refer to Macbeth.
218   *dam :* mother.
219   *fell :* cruel.
       swoop : stroke (Macduff is still
       thinking of Macbeth as a bird—
       'hell-kite'—that 'swoops' down on its
       prey).
       Dispute : bear.
222   *cannot but remember :* cannot help
       remembering.
       such things : i.e. his wife and
       children.
225   *struck for thee :* killed for your
       faults.
       Naught that I am : although I am
       nothing.
226   *demerits :* failings.
228   *whetstone :* the stone used for
       sharpening knives and swords.
229   *blunt . . . it :* do not let your heart
       become insensitive, but let it be angry.
230   *play . . . eyes :* my eyes could play
       the part of a woman (and weep).
231   *braggart :* boaster (who threatens
       more than he can do).
232   *intermission :* interval (between
       now and the time he sees Macbeth).
       front to front : face to face.
234-5 If I let him escape, it will serve
       me right if heaven forgives him too.
236   *power :* force (army).
237   We need nothing except to say
       goodbye.
239   *instruments :* weapons. Malcolm
       claims that the forces of good are
       arming themselves to aid him, just as
       Lady Macbeth called for the ministers
       of evil to help her with the murder of
       Duncan (*1,* 5, 47-9).
       cheer : comfort.

Act 5

Act 5   scene 1

Lady Macbeth suffers from a guilty conscience. She walks in her sleep, and dreams that she and her husband are murdering King Duncan.

1   *watched*: stayed awake.

4   *the field*: i.e. the battlefield.
5   *night-gown*: dressing-gown.
6   *closet*: cupboard.

8   *fast*: sound.

9   *perturbation in nature*: upheaval in life.
10 *do ... watching*: act as if she were awake.
11 *slumbery agitation*: activity whilst sleeping.

14 *report after her*: repeat behind her back.

15 *meet*: proper.

18 *guise*: appearance.

20 *close*: hidden.

Scene 1 *Dunsinane. A room in the castle*

A Doctor of Physic *and a* Waiting-Gentlewoman

Doctor
I have two nights watched with you, but can perceive no truth in your report. When was it she last walked?

Gentlewoman
Since his majesty went into the field, I have seen
5 her rise from her bed, throw her night-gown upon her, unlock her closet, take forth paper, fold it, write upon 't, read it, afterwards seal it, and again return to bed; yet all this while in a most fast sleep.

Doctor
A great perturbation in nature, to receive at once
10 the benefit of sleep and do the effects of watching! In this slumbery agitation, besides her walking and other actual performances, what, at any time, have you heard her say?

Gentlewoman
That, sir, which I will not report after her.

Doctor
15 You may to me, and 'tis most meet you should.

Gentlewoman
Neither to you nor any one, having no witness to confirm my speech.

Enter Lady Macbeth *with a candle*
Lo you! here she comes. This is her very guise; and, upon my life, fast asleep. Observe her; stand
20 close.

Doctor
How came she by that light?

Gentlewoman
Why, it stood by her: she has light by her continually; 'tis her command.

Doctor
You see, her eyes are open.
Gentlewoman
25 Ay, but their sense is shut.
Doctor
What is it she does now? Look, how she rubs her
hands.
Gentlewoman
It is an accustomed action with her, to seem thus
washing her hands. I have known her continue in
30 this a quarter of an hour.
Lady Macbeth
Yet here's a spot.
Doctor
Hark! she speaks. I will set down what comes from
her, to satisfy my remembrance the more strongly.
Lady Macbeth
Out, damned spot! out, I say! One; two: why, then
35 'tis time to do 't. Hell is murky! Fie, my lord—fie!
a soldier, and afeard? What need we fear who
knows it, when none can call our power to account?
Yet who would have thought the old man to have
had so much blood in him?
Doctor
40 Do you mark that?
Lady Macbeth
The Thane of Fife had a wife: where is she now?
What, will these hands ne'er be clean? No more
o' that, my lord, no more o' that: you mar all with
this starting.
Doctor
45 Go to, go to; you have known what you should not.
Gentlewoman
She has spoke what she should not, I am sure of
that: Heaven knows what she has known.
Lady Macbeth
Here's the smell of the blood still: all the perfumes
of Arabia will not sweeten this little hand. Oh!
50 oh! oh!

---

25 *sense*: understanding.

32 *set*: write.
33 *satisfy my remembrance*: confirm my
    memory.

36 *afeard*: afraid.
37 *none . . . account*: no one will be able
    to make us confess how we got this
    power.

44 *starting*: jumpiness.

45 *Go to*: Alas!

51 *sorely charged :* grievously burdened.

Doctor
What a sigh is there! The heart is sorely charged.
Gentlewoman
I would not have such a heart in my bosom for the
dignity of the whole body.
Doctor
Well, well, well.
Gentlewoman
55 Pray God it be, sir.
Doctor

56 *beyond my practice :* too serious for me
to treat.

This disease is beyond my practice: yet I have
known those which have walked in their sleep who
have died holily in their beds.
Lady Macbeth
Wash your hands, put on your night-gown; look
60 not so pale. I tell you yet again, Banquo's buried;
he cannot come out on 's grave.

61 *on 's :* of his.

Doctor
Even so?
Lady Macbeth
To bed, to bed: there's knocking at the gate. Come,
come, come, come, give me your hand. What's
65 done cannot be undone. To bed, to bed, to bed.
[*Exit*
Doctor
Will she go now to bed?
Gentlewoman
Directly.
Doctor

68 *whisperings :* rumours.
abroad : about, at large.

70 *discharge :* confide.

71 *divine :* priest.

Foul whisperings are abroad. Unnatural deeds
Do breed unnatural troubles; infected minds
70 To their deaf pillows will discharge their secrets.
More needs she the divine than the physician.
God, God forgive us all! Look after her;

73 *means of all annoyance :* anything she
might use to harm herself.

74 *still :* always.
75 *mated :* bewildered.

Remove from her the means of all annoyance,
And still keep eyes upon her. So, good-night:
75 My mind she has mated, and amaz'd my sight.
I think, but dare not speak.
Gentlewoman   Good-night, good doctor.
[*Exeunt*

Act 5   scene 2

A section of the army marches towards Dunsinane. The leaders discuss their enemy, Macbeth, who is showing signs of panic.

sd   *colours :* regimental banners.

3   *Revenges :* desire for revenge.
3–5   Their causes are powerful enough to rouse ('Excite') a dead ('mortified') man to come to the bloodshed and answer the call to arms ('alarm').

8   *file :* list.

10   *unrough :* beardless.
11   Show that they have now reached manhood.

15–16   These lines could mean *either* 'He cannot discipline his rebellious ("distemper'd") kingdom', *or* 'He cannot restrain his own diseased ("distemper'd") passions'.
18   Now every minute more men revolt from him, and this rebukes him for his own rebellion.
19–20   They obey him because he is their commander, not because they love him.

23   *pester'd senses :* troubled nerves.
    to recoil and start : to be jumpy.
24–5   His whole being is revolted by itself.

Scene 2 *Countryside near Dunsinane*

Enter, with drum and colours, Menteith,
Caithness, Angus, Lennox, *and* Soldiers

Menteith
The English power is near, led on by Malcolm,
His uncle Siward, and the good Macduff.
Revenges burn in them; for their dear causes
Would to the bleeding and the grim alarm
5 Excite the mortified man.
Angus   Near Birnam wood
Shall we well meet them; that way are they coming.
Caithness
Who knows if Donalbain be with his brother?
Lennox
For certain, sir, he is not: I have a file
Of all the gentry: there is Siward's son,
10 And many unrough youths that even now
Protest their first of manhood.
Menteith   What does the tyrant?
Caithness
Great Dunsinane he strongly fortifies.
Some say he's mad; others, that lesser hate him
Do call it valiant fury; but, for certain,
15 He cannot buckle his distemper'd cause
Within the belt of rule.
Angus   Now does he feel
His secret murders sticking on his hands;
Now minutely revolts upbraid his faith-breach;
Those he commands move only in command,
20 Nothing in love; now does he feel his title
Hang loose about him, like a giant's robe
Upon a dwarfish thief.
Menteith   Who then shall blame
His pester'd senses to recoil and start,
When all that is within him does condemn
25 Itself for being there?

Caithness   Well, march we on,
To give obedience where 'tis truly ow'd;
Meet we the medicine of the sickly weal,
And with him pour we in our country's purge,
Each drop of us.
Lennox   Or so much as it needs
30 To dew the sovereign flower and drown the weeds.
Make we our march towards Birnam.
                    [*Exeunt, marching*

Scene 3 *Dunsinane. A room in the castle*

Enter Macbeth, Doctor, *and* Attendants
Macbeth
Bring me no more reports; let them fly all:
Till Birnam wood remove to Dunsinane
I cannot taint with fear. What's the boy Malcolm?
Was he not born of woman? The spirits that know
5 All mortal consequences have pronounc'd me thus:
'Fear not, Macbeth; no man that's born of woman
Shall e'er have power upon thee.' Then fly, false thanes,
And mingle with the English epicures:
The mind I sway by, and the heart I bear
10 Shall never sag with doubt nor shake with fear.

Enter a Servant
The devil damn thee black, thou cream-fac'd loon!
Where gott'st thou that goose look?
Servant
There is ten thousand—
Macbeth   Geese, villain?
Servant   Soldiers, sir.
Macbeth
Go, prick thy face, and over-red thy fear,
15 Thou lily-liver'd boy. What soldiers, patch?
Death of thy soul! those linen cheeks of thine
Are counsellors to fear. What soldiers, whey-face?
Servant
The English force, so please you.

---

27 *the medicine* : the doctor (i.e. Malcolm).
   weal : land.
28 Let us, with Malcolm, pour out every
   drop of our blood to cleanse our
   country. (A widely-prescribed
   treatment for diseases was blood-
   letting—drawing off some of the
   patient's blood.)
30 *dew* : water.

Act 5   scene 3
Macbeth tries to comfort himself by
recalling the witches' prophecies as he
is told of the approaching armies. He
discusses his wife's illness with the
Doctor, and then goes off to battle.
1 *them* : i.e. the thanes.
2 *remove* : moves.
3 *taint* : go rotten.
5 *mortal consequences* : human causes
   and effects.
   have pronounc'd me : have spoken
   about me.
8 *English epicures* : soft-living English.
9 *sway* : rule myself.

11 *loon* : fool.

14 *over-red thy fear* : colour your white
   face (white through fear) red with the
   blood from the pricks.
15 *lily-liver'd* : coward—because the
   blood had drained from his liver, the
   seat of courage, and left it white like
   a lily.
   patch : clown.
16 *linen* : i.e. white.
17 *counsellors* : persuaders.
   whey : the thin white liquid that is
   left when milk has curdled.

Macbeth
Take thy face hence.   [*Exit* Servant
                        Seyton! I am sick at heart

20 When I behold—Seyton, I say!—This push
     Will cheer me ever or disseat me now.
     I have liv'd long enough: my way of life
     Is fall'n into the sere, the yellow leaf;
     And that which should accompany old age,
25 As honour, love, obedience, troops of friends,
     I must not look to have; but, in their stead,
     Curses, not loud but deep, mouth-honour, breath,
     Which the poor heart would fain deny, and dare
        not.
     Seyton!

                 Enter Seyton
      Seyton
30 What is your gracious pleasure?
      Macbeth   What news more?
      Seyton
     All is confirm'd, my lord, which was reported.
      Macbeth
     I'll fight till from my bones my flesh be hack'd.
     Give me my armour.
      Seyton   'Tis not needed yet.
      Macbeth
     I'll put it on.
35 Send out more horses, skirr the country round;
     Hang those that talk of fear. Give me mine armour.
     How does your patient, doctor?
      Doctor   Not so sick, my lord,
     As she is troubled with thick-coming fancies,
     That keep her from her rest.
      Macbeth   Cure her of that:
40 Canst thou not minister to a mind diseas'd,
     Pluck from the memory a rooted sorrow,
     Raze out the written troubles of the brain,
     And with some sweet oblivious antidote
     Cleanse the stuff'd bosom of that perilous stuff
45 Which weighs upon the heart?

---

20 *behold.* He does not complete the
    sentence.
    push : attack.
21 *cheer :* comfort; but there is also a pun
    with 'chair' meaning 'enthrone'.
    disseat : de-throne.
22 *my way of life :* the course of my life.
23 *the sere :* the withered state.
27 *mouth-honour :* lip-service.
28 *fain deny :* wish to withold.

35 *skirr :* scour, move swiftly.

38 *thick-coming :* crowding in on each
    other.

40 *minister to :* treat.
41 *rooted :* deeply embedded.
42 *Raze :* erase.
    written : imprinted.
43 *oblivious :* causing forgetfulness.
44 *stuff'd bosom :* burdened heart.
45 *weighs upon :* distresses.

47 *I'll none of it :* I won't have
anything to do with it (because it
is useless).

50 *dispatch :* get on with it!
 cast : analyse.
51 *water :* urine.
52 *pristine :* as good as new.
53-4 I would praise you so loudly that
my praises would echo and re-echo.
54 *Pull 't off :* Some piece of armour
does not fit properly, and he orders
Seyton to take it off and (line 58)
bring it after him.
55 Rhubarb and senna are both
'purgative' (laxative) drugs.
57 *preparation :* i.e. for war.

59 *bane :* destruction.

61 *clear :* free.
62 *Profit :* Doctors were noted for
avarice.

Act 5   scene 4

Malcolm and his soldiers draw closer
to Dunsinane.

2 *chambers :* bedrooms—i.e. where
we can sleep in safety.
 nothing : not at all.

Doctor   Therein the patient
Must minister to himself.
  Macbeth
Throw physic to the dogs; I'll none of it.
Come, put mine armour on; give me my staff.
Seyton, send out.—Doctor, the thanes fly from
 me.—
50 Come, sir, dispatch.—If thou couldst, doctor, cast
The water of my land, find her disease,
And purge it to a sound and pristine health,
I would applaud thee to the very echo,
That should applaud again.—Pull 't off, I say.—
55 What rhubarb, senna, or what purgative drug
Would scour these English hence? Hear'st thou of
 them?
  Doctor
Ay, my good lord; your royal preparation
Makes us hear something.
  Macbeth   Bring it after me.
I will not be afraid of death and bane
60 Till Birnam forest come to Dunsinane.
  Doctor
[*Aside*] Were I from Dunsinane away and clear,
Profit again should hardly draw me here. [*Exeunt*

Scene 4 *Near Birnam Wood*

   Enter, with drum and colours, Malcolm,
   Old Siward *and his* Son, Macduff,
   Menteith, Caithness, Angus, Lennox,
   Ross, *and* Soldiers, *marching*
  Malcolm
Cousins, I hope the days are near at hand
That chambers will be safe.
  Menteith   We doubt it nothing.
  Siward
What wood is this before us?
  Menteith
The wood of Birnam.

6-7   *shadow . . . host :* conceal the size
of our army.

7-8   *make . . . us :* make those who spy
on us give a false report.

9   *no other :* nothing else.

10   *endure :* allow.

11   *our setting down :* i.e. in a siege.

12   *advantage to be gone :* opportunity
to escape.

13   *more and less :* high and low in
rank.

given . . . revolt : rebelled against
him.

14   *constrained things :* miserable
conscripts.

15-16   *Let . . . event :* let us wait to give
an opinion until after the event.

18   *due :* proper (because the decision
will be made by the result of the battle).

19   What we can claim to possess, and
what we lack.

20-1   Speculation about what will
happen is based on uncertain hopes,
but actual fighting ('strokes') must
decide ('arbitrate') the outcome
('issue') and make it certain. (Like
Macduff, Siward warns Malcolm not
to be too optimistic.)

22   *advance :* carry on with.

Act 5   scene 5

The battle is at its height when Seyton
brings news to Macbeth that his wife
has just died. Macbeth does not grieve,
because he feels that life is meaningless.
A Messenger tells him that Birnam
Wood is moving towards the castle.

4   *ague :* fever.

5   *forc'd :* reinforced.

Malcolm

5 Let every soldier hew him down a bough
And bear 't before him: thereby shall we shadow
The numbers of our host, and make discovery
Err in report of us.
Soldiers   It shall be done.
Siward
We learn no other but the confident tyrant
10 Keeps still in Dunsinane, and will endure
Our setting down before 't.
Malcolm   'Tis his main hope;
For where there is advantage to be gone,
Both more and less have given him the revolt,
And none serve with him but constrained things
15 Whose hearts are absent too.
Macduff   Let our just censures
Attend the true event, and put we on
Industrious soldiership.
Siward   The time approaches
That will with due decision make us know
What we shall say we have, and what we owe.
20 Thoughts speculative their unsure hopes relate,
But certain issue strokes must arbitrate,
Towards which advance the war.

                              [*Exeunt, marching*

Scene 5 *Inside the castle*

        Enter, with a drum and colours, Macbeth,
        Seyton, *and* Soldiers
Macbeth
Hang out our banners on the outward walls;
The cry is still, 'They come'. Our castle's strength
Will laugh a siege to scorn; here let them lie
Till famine and the ague eat them up;
5 Were they not forc'd with those that should be ours,

6   *dareful :* defiantly.

We might have met them dareful, beard to beard,
And beat them backward home.

[*A cry of women within*
What is that noise?

Seyton
It is the cry of women, my good lord.   [*Exit*

Macbeth
I have almost forgot the taste of fears.
10 The time has been my senses would have cool'd
To hear a night-shriek, and my fell of hair
Would at a dismal treatise rouse and stir
As life were in 't. I have supp'd full with horrors;
Direness, familiar to my slaughterous thoughts,
15 Cannot once start me.

10   *cool'd :* frozen.
11   *night-shriek :* cry at night.
       fell : fleece, scalp.
12   *dismal treatise :* frightening story.
13   *As :* as if.
14   *Direness :* horror.
15   *Cannot . . . me :* can never alarm me.

Enter Seyton

Wherefore was that cry?

Seyton
The queen, my lord, is dead.

Macbeth
She should have died hereafter;
There would have been a time for such a word.
To-morrow, and to-morrow, and to-morrow,
20 Creeps in this petty pace from day to day,
To the last syllable of recorded time;
And all our yesterdays have lighted fools
The way to dusty death. Out, out, brief candle!
Life's but a walking shadow, a poor player
25 That struts and frets his hour upon the stage,
And then is heard no more; it is a tale
Told by an idiot, full of sound and fury,
Signifying nothing.

17   She would have died at some time
     or other.
18   The word would have to be spoken
     at some time.
20   One day creeps after another at
     this trivial rate.
21   Until the very end of time—the
     last syllable written in the book.
22-3 Every day that has passed has done
     no more than give light to fools on
     their way to death.
23   *candle :* i.e. Life.

√

Enter a Messenger
Thou com'st to use thy tongue; thy story quickly.

Messenger
30 Gracious my lord,
I should report that which I say I saw,
But know not how to do it.

Macbeth   Well, say, sir.

Messenger
As I did stand my watch upon the hill,

31   *should :* ought to.
     I say I saw : I declare I saw.

33   *watch :* guard.

34   *anon :* suddenly.

40   *cling :* shrink up.
     sooth : the truth.
41   *as much :* the same.
42   *pull in resolution :* check my
     determination.
43   *equivocation :* double dealing.
44   Whose lies become truths.

47   *avouches :* affirms.
48   I can neither escape nor stay here.
49   *the sun :* i.e. life.
50   *estate o' the world :* the whole creation.
51   *wrack :* wreck.
52   *harness :* armour.

I look'd toward Birnam, and anon, methought,
35 The wood began to move.
> **Macbeth**   Liar and slave!
> **Messenger**
Let me endure your wrath if 't be not so:
Within this three mile you may see it coming;
I say, a moving grove.
> **Macbetn**   If thou speak'st false,
Upon the next tree shalt thou hang alive,
40 Till famine cling thee; if thy speech be sooth,
I care not if thou dost for me as much.
I pull in resolution, and begin
To doubt the equivocation of the fiend
That lies like truth; 'Fear not, till Birnam wood
45 Do come to Dunsinane', and now a wood
Comes toward Dunsinane. Arm, arm, and out!
If this which he avouches does appear,
There is nor flying hence, nor tarrying here.
I 'gin to be aweary of the sun,
50 And wish the estate o' the world were now undone.
Ring the alarum-bell! Blow, wind! come, wrack!
At least we'll die with harness on our back.
>   [*Exeunt*

Act 5   scene 6
Battle is commenced.

2   *show like those you are :* appear as
yourselves (i.e. soldiers).

6   *order :* plan of campaign.

7   *power :* army.

10   *harbingers :* heralds.

Scene 6   *A plain before the castle*

> *Enter, with drum and colours,* Malcolm,
> *Old* Siward, Macduff, *and their Army,*
> *with boughs*
> **Malcolm**
Now near enough; your leafy screens throw down,
And show like those you are. You, worthy uncle,
Shall, with my cousin, your right noble son,
Lead our first battle; worthy Macduff and we
5 Shall take upon 's what else remains to do,
According to our order.
> **Siward**   Fare you well.
Do we but find the tyrant's power tonight,
Let us be beaten, if we cannot fight.
> **Macduff**
Make all our trumpets speak; give them all breath,
10 Those clamorous harbingers of blood and death.
>   [*Exeunt*

Act 5   scene 7

The battle continues throughout this scene. Macbeth meets young Siward, and kills him. Macduff hurries across the stage in search of Macbeth. They fight. Victory is proclaimed, and Malcolm is king.

1   *tied me to a stake*. A bear was tied to a post and attacked by dogs in the sport of 'bear-baiting'.

Scene 7 *Another part of the plain*

Alarums. Enter Macbeth

Macbeth
They have tied me to a stake; I cannot fly,
But bear-like I must fight the course. What's he
That was not born of woman? Such a one
Am I to fear, or none.

Enter Young Siward

Young Siward
5 What is thy name?

Macbeth   Thou'lt be afraid to hear it.

Young Siward
No; though thou call'st thyself a hotter name
Than any is in hell.

Macbeth   My name's Macbeth.

Young Siward
The devil himself could not pronounce a title
More hateful to mine ear.

Macbeth   No, nor more fearful.

Young Siward

10 Thou liest, abhorred tyrant; with my sword
I'll prove the lie thou speak'st.

[*They fight and Young* Siward *is slain*

Macbeth   Thou wast born of woman:
But swords I smile at, weapons laugh to scorn,
Brandish'd by man that's of a woman born.   [*Exit*

Alarums. Enter Macduff

Macduff

That way the noise is. Tyrant, show thy face:
15 If thou be'st slain and with no stroke of mine,
My wife and children's ghosts will haunt me still.
I cannot strike at wretched kerns, whose arms
Are hir'd to bear their staves: either thou, Macbeth,
Or else my sword with an unbatter'd edge
20 I sheathe again undeeded. There thou shouldst be;
By this great clatter, one of greatest note
Seems bruited. Let me find him, fortune!
And more I beg not.   [*Exit. Alarums*

Enter Malcolm *and Old* Siward

Siward

This way, my lord; the castle's gently render'd:
25 The tyrant's people on both sides do fight;
The noble thanes do bravely in the war;
The day almost itself professes yours,
And little is to do.

Malcolm   We have met with foes
That strike beside us.

Siward   Enter, sir, the castle.

[*Exeunt. Alarums*

Enter Macbeth

Macbeth

30 Why should I play the Roman fool, and die
On mine own sword? whiles I see lives, the gashes
Do better upon them.

Enter Macduff

Macduff   Turn, hell-hound, turn!

Macbeth

Of all men else I have avoided thee:
But get thee back, my soul is too much charg'd
35 With blood of thine already.

---

11 *prove the lie*: prove it to be a lie.

16 *still*: for ever.
17 *kerns*: mercenaries (see note to *1, 2, 13*).
18 *staves*: spear-shafts.
20 *undeeded*: not having performed any deeds.
21 *note*: importance.
22 *bruited*: reported.

24 *gently render'd*: peaceably surrendered.

27 You have almost won the day.

29 *strike beside us*: fight on our side.

30 *Roman*. The Romans thought it dishonourable to be captured, and when they knew they were defeated they committed suicide.

34 *charg'd*: guilty.

37   *Than . . . out :* than words can say.

38   *intrenchant :* incapable of being cut, invulnerable.
39   *impress :* make an impression on.

41   *must not :* is not destined to be.

42   *Despair :* despair of.

45   *Untimely :* prematurely; Macduff was delivered by a caesarean operation.

47   *cow'd . . . man :* subdued my spirit.
48   *juggling :* deceptive (they played with words as a juggler plays with balls).
49   *palter :* trifle.
      in a double sense : using words with two meanings, ambiguously.
50-1 Keep their promise by the sound of it, but break it when we do not get what we hoped for.
53   *show . . . time :* spectacle of the age.
55   Painted on a sign which is hung from a pole.
      underwrit : written underneath.

58   *baited :* taunted.

60   *oppos'd :* fighting against me.
61   *try the last :* fight to the end.

63sd *Retreat. Flourish :* trumpets give a call that signifies surrender; then other trumpets (Malcolm's) sound the call of triumph.

64   *we miss :* who are absent.

Macduff   I have no words;
My voice is in my sword, thou bloodier villain
Than terms can give thee out!   [*They fight*
   Macbeth   Thou losest labour:
As easy may'st thou the intrenchant air
With thy keen sword impress, as make me bleed:
40 Let fall thy blade on vulnerable crests;
I bear a charmed life, which must not yield
To one of woman born.
   Macduff   Despair thy charm;
And let the angel whom thou still hast serv'd
Tell thee, Macduff was from his mother's womb
45 Untimely ripp'd.
   Macbeth
Accursed be that tongue that tells me so,
For it hath cow'd my better part of man:
And be these juggling fiends no more believ'd,
That palter with us in a double sense;
50 That keep the word of promise to our ear,
And break it to our hope. I'll not fight with thee.
   Macduff
Then yield thee, coward,
And live to be the show and gaze o' the time:
We'll have thee, as our rarer monsters are,
55 Painted upon a pole, and underwrit,
'Here may you see the tyrant.'
   Macbeth   I will not yield,
To kiss the ground before young Malcolm's feet,
And to be baited with the rabble's curse.
Though Birnam wood be come to Dunsinane,
60 And thou oppos'd, being of no woman born,
Yet I will try the last. Before my body
I throw my warlike shield: lay on, Macduff,
And damn'd be him that first cries, 'Hold, enough!'
        [*Exeunt, fighting*

Retreat. Flourish. Enter, with drum and colours, Malcolm, Old Siward, Ross, Thanes, *and* Soldiers
   Malcolm
I would the friends we miss were safe arriv'd.

65 *go off :* be killed.
    by these : judging by these men I
    see here.

68 *soldier's debt :* i.e. he has been
    killed in action.

71 In the post where he fought without
    flinching.
73 *brought off the field :* his body has
    been carried from the battlefield.
73–5 You must not mourn for him as
    much as he deserves, because then you
    would never stop mourning.
75 *before :* on the front of his body (he
    was not running away when he was
    killed).
76 I give him as a soldier to God.

77 *hairs.* Siward makes a brave pun
    on 'heirs'.
79 *his knell is knoll'd :* his funeral bell
    has been rung (and there is no more
    to say).
81 *parted :* died.
    score : debts.

84 *time :* age.
85 *pearl :* jewels (i.e. the nobles).
86–7 They salute you in their hearts as
    I do, and I want them to say aloud
    with me.

Siward
65 Some must go off; and yet, by these I see,
So great a day as this is cheaply bought.
Malcolm
Macduff is missing, and your noble son.
Ross
Your son, my lord, has paid a soldier's debt :
He only liv'd but till he was a man ;
70 The which no sooner had his prowess confirm'd
In the unshrinking station where he fought,
But like a man he died.
Siward   Then he is dead?
Ross
Ay, and brought off the field. Your cause of sorrow
Must not be measur'd by his worth, for then
75 It hath no end.
Siward   Had he his hurts before?
Ross
Ay, on the front.
Siward   Why then, God's soldier be he !
Had I as many sons as I have hairs,
I would not wish them to a fairer death :
And so, his knell is knoll'd.
Malcolm   He's worth more sorrow,
80 And that I'll spend for him.
Siward   He's worth no more ;
They say he parted well, and paid his score :
And so, God be with him ! Here comes newer
comfort.

Enter Macduff, *with* Macbeth's *head*
Macduff
Hail, king ! for so thou art. Behold, where stands
The usurper's cursed head : the time is free.
85 I see thee compass'd with thy kingdom's pearl,
That speak my salutation in their minds ;
Whose voices I desire aloud with mine :
Hail, King of Scotland !
All   Hail, King of Scotland !
[*Flourish*

90 *reckon . . . loves :* repay each one of you individually for your loyalty.
91 *even :* equal (in obligation).

94 *would be :* ought to be.
planted . . . time : started now, just as a new age has begun.

97 *Producing forth :* bringing out.
ministers : agents.

99 *by self and violent hands :* by her own violent hands.

100 *what needful else :* whatever else is necessary.

101 *calls upon us :* demands our attention.
grace of Grace : grace of God.

102 *in measure, time, and place :* in the proper order, at the right time, and in the proper place. Malcolm has brought harmony back to Scotland.

Malcolm
We shall not spend a large expense of time
90 Before we reckon with your several loves,
And make us even with you. My thanes and
    kinsmen,
Henceforth be earls, the first that ever Scotland
In such an honour nam'd. What's more to do,
Which would be planted newly with the time—
95 As calling home our exil'd friends abroad
That fled the snares of watchful tyranny;
Producing forth the cruel ministers
Of this dead butcher and his fiend-like queen,
Who, as 'tis thought, by self and violent hands
100 Took off her life—this, and what needful else
That calls upon us, by the grace of Grace,
We will perform in measure, time, and place.
So, thanks to all at once, and to each one,
Whom we invite to see us crown'd at Scone.
                              [*Flourish. Exeunt*

Examinations

I know that many of you will have been studying *Macbeth* for examination purposes, and I want now to offer some suggestions about the techniques of answering examination questions.

First of all, you must know the play well: that is, you must know what happens in it, what the characters are like, and what the words mean. Then, the most important rule in any kind of examination is: *answer the question*. You will always have far more information to offer than the question asks for; but the purpose of the examination is not simply to test what you know. The examiners want to find out how well you can *use* what you know—how you can select information that is relevant to the question, and how you can organize your material into a coherent and logical argument.

There are two kinds of question that may be presented to you, 'context' questions, and essay questions. Your answers to both of these should contain enough—and no more! The questions that I have chosen to try to answer here are taken from a recent examination paper.

Context questions These questions present you with short passages from the play, and ask questions about them. Usually you have to make a choice of passages; there may be five on the paper, and you are asked to choose three. Be very sure that you know how many passages you should choose. Study the ones offered to you, and select those that you feel most certain of.

Question

> Then comes my fit again; I had else been perfect;
> Whole as the marble, founded as the rock,
> As broad and general as the casing air;
> But now I am cabin'd, cribb'd, confin'd, bound in
> To saucy doubts and fears.

(i) By whom are the lines spoken, and on what occasion?

(ii) What news has the speaker just received, and from whom?

(iii) What question does the speaker go on to ask, and what reply does he receive?

Suggested answer

(i) Macbeth is speaking, at the state banquet.

(ii) He has been told that Banquo has been murdered but that Fleance has escaped. One of the Murderers.

(iii) Whether Banquo has really been killed. That he is dead in a ditch.

Question

> With this, there grows
> In my most ill-compos'd affection, such
> A staunchless avarice that, were I king,
> I should cut off the nobles for their lands,
> Desire his jewels, and this other's house.

(i) Who is the speaker of these lines? To whom are they addressed?

(ii) What does the person addressed say in response to these words?

(iii) Why does the speaker accuse himself? What effect does his self-accusation finally have?

Suggested answer

(i) Malcolm. To Macduff.

(ii) Macduff replies that the king of Scotland has enough property of his own to satisfy Malcolm's greed.

(iii) To test Macduff's loyalty and to make sure that he is not a spy sent by Macbeth. Macduff is disgusted and distressed about the future of Scotland.

Essay questions These questions always give you a specific topic to discuss. They *never* want you to tell the story of the whole play—so don't: the examiner has read the play, and does not need to be reminded of it. Give him only what he asks for.

Question

Describe and illustrate the ways in which the characters of Macbeth and Lady Macbeth are revealed from the time that Lady Macbeth receives her husband's letter in Act I up to the murder of Duncan, paying special attention to the differences between them.

Suggested approach to an answer

First, make a list of the material you can draw on for this answer; then make a plan. The plan should be no more than an outline: you do not have time to write a rough draft of your essay and copy it out later. Remember that the question is asking for the *ways* in which the characters are revealed, as well as for the characters themselves. Your plan might look like this:

Macbeth	Lady Macbeth
ambition and unwillingness to do evil; described in wife's soliloquy	desire to be inhuman and evil, revealed in own soliloquy
loyalty to king, sense of duties, revealed in own soliloquy	hypocrisy, shown when she tells M to deceive the king
sense of sin, before and after murder of Duncan, revealed in soliloquy and conversation with wife	scorn and bullying when she talks to M
	need to have a drink before murder of Duncan
	failure to appreciate morally what murder means

Is this complete?

Read through the question again, before writing your answer. This question asks you to pay special attention to the differences between Macbeth and his wife, so **add**

Contrast: Macbeth's ambition and his wife's
   Macbeth's reaction to his bloody hands, and Lady
   Macbeth's reaction

Can you remember any of the actual words of the play? If you can, it will help you to make your points more strongly, and show the examiner that you have indeed studied *the play*, and not just a prose account of the action and characters. But quotations must always be relevant. If they are not relevant, it is a waste of time writing them out; you will get no marks for this.

Specimen questions

1. Context questions.

(a) Do not muse at me, my most worthy friends;
I have a strange infirmity, which is nothing
To those that know me. Come, love and health to all:

Then, I'll sit down. Give me some wine, fill full;
I drink to the general joy of the whole table.

(i) Who is speaking, and on what occasion?
(ii) What has caused him to behave strangely?
(iii) What happens immediately after these lines?

(b)   Art thou afeard
To be the same in thine own act and valour
As thou art in desire? Wouldst thou have that
Which thou esteem'st the ornament of life,
And live a coward in thine own esteem?

(i) Who is speaking, and to whom?
(ii) What is the person addressed afraid to do?
(iii) What effect does this speech have on the person
addressed?

(c)   Wisdom! to leave his wife, to leave his babes,
His mansion and his titles, in a place
From whence himself does fly? He loves us not,
He wants the natural touch.

(i) Who is speaking, and to whom?
(ii) What person is being spoken about?
(iii) What happens to the speaker shortly after
these lines have been spoken?

(d)   A heavy summons lies like lead upon me,
And yet I would not sleep: merciful powers!
Restrain in me the cursed thoughts that nature
Gives way to in repose. Give me my sword!

(i) Who is the speaker? Who accompanies him?
(ii) Why is he unwilling to sleep?
(iii) Why does he ask for his sword?

(e)   Have you considered of my speeches? Know
That it was he, in the times past, which held you
So under fortune, which you thought had been
Our innocent self.

(i) Who is speaking? To whom does he speak?
(ii) Who is the 'he' referred to?
(iii) What does the speaker want his hearers to do?

(f)   did he not straight,
In pious rage the two delinquents tear,
That were the slaves of drink, and thralls of sleep?
Was not that nobly done? Ay, and wisely, too;
For 'twould have anger'd any heart alive
To hear the men deny't.

(i) Who is speaking, and about whom?
(ii) Who are the 'two delinquents'?
(iii) What would they have denied?

(g)   That which hath made them drunk hath made me
bold.
What hath quench'd them hath given me fire. Hark!
Peace!
It was the owl that shriek'd, the fatal bellman
Which gives the stern'st good-night. He is about it.

(i) Who is speaking?
(ii) What is the speaker listening for?
(iii) Who comes on to the stage after these lines?
What has he done?

(h)   We hear our bloody cousins are bestow'd
In England and in Ireland, not confessing
Their cruel parricide, filling their hearers
With strange invention. But of that tomorrow,
When, therewithal, we shall have cause of state
Craving us jointly.

(i) Who is speaking, and to whom does he speak?
(ii) Who are the 'bloody cousins'?
(iii) Will the person addressed attend the meeting
tomorrow? Why?

2   How important is the influence of Lady Macbeth on her
husband?

3   What have you learned from *Macbeth* about the
Elizabethan concept of the king?

4   Describe the character of Macduff, and show how
Shakespeare wins respect and approval for him.

5   Give an account of the part played by the supernatural
in *Macbeth*.

6   We will establish our estate upon
Our eldest, Malcolm.

Explain why this is an important announcement.

7　Compare and contrast Lady Macbeth and Lady Macduff.

8　What means does Shakespeare use to create 'atmosphere' in *Macbeth*?

9　At the beginning of the play Macbeth writes to his wife as 'my dearest partner of greatness'. How does their relationship change during the play?

10　Give an account of the function of Ross in the play.

11　Describe how Duncan rewards good and bad service.

12　Discuss the importance of sleep in *Macbeth*.

13　Is there any comedy in *Macbeth*? Is it necessary?

14　'Everyone in the play either suspects, or is himself suspected.' Show how true this is.

15　Do you feel any pity for Macbeth's 'fiend-like queen'?

Elizabeth I was Queen of England when Shakespeare was born in 1564. He was the son of a tradesman who made and sold gloves in the small town of Stratford-upon-Avon, and he was educated at the grammar school in that town. Shakespeare did not go to university when he left school, but worked, perhaps, in his father's business. When he was eighteen he married Anne Hathaway, who became the mother of his daughter, Susanna, in 1583, and of twins in 1585.

There is nothing exciting, or even unusual, in this story; and from 1585 until 1592 there are no documents that can tell us anything at all about Shakespeare. But we have learned that in 1592 he was known in London, and that he had become both an actor and a playwright.

We do not know when Shakespeare wrote his first play, and indeed we are not sure of the order in which he wrote his works. If you look on page 95 at the list of his writings and their approximate dates, you will see how he started by writing plays on subjects taken from the history of England. No doubt this was partly because he was always an intensely patriotic man—but he was also a very shrewd business-man. He could see that the theatre audiences enjoyed being shown their own history, and it was certain that he would make a profit from this kind of drama.

The plays in the next group are mainly comedies, with romantic love stories of young people who fall in love with one another, and at the end of the play marry and live happily ever after.

At the end of the sixteenth century the happiness disappears, and Shakespeare's plays become melancholy, bitter, and tragic. This change may have been caused by some sadness in the writer's life (one of his twins died in 1596). Shakespeare, however, was not the only writer whose works at this time were very serious. The whole of England was facing a crisis. Queen Elizabeth I was growing old. She was greatly loved, and the people were sad to think she must soon die; they were also afraid, for the Queen had never married, and so there was no child to succeed her.

When James I came to the throne in 1603, Shakespeare continued to write serious drama—the great tragedies and the plays based on Roman history (such as *Julius Caesar*) for which he is most famous. Finally, before he retired from the theatre, he wrote another set of comedies. These all have the same theme: they tell of happiness which is lost, and then found again.

Shakespeare returned from London to Stratford, his home town. He was rich and successful, and he owned one of the biggest houses in the town. He died in 1616.

Shakespeare also wrote two long poems, and a collection of sonnets. The sonnets describe two love-affairs, but we do not know who the lovers were. Although there are many public documents concerned with his career as a writer and a business-man, Shakespeare has hidden his personal life from us. A nineteenth-century poet, Matthew Arnold, addressed Shakespeare in a poem, and wrote 'We ask and ask—Thou smilest, and art still'.

There is not even a trustworthy portrait of the world's greatest dramatist.

Approximate order of composition of Shakespeare's works

Period	Comedies	History plays	Tragedies	Poems
I 1594	Comedy of Errors Taming of the Shrew Two Gentlemen of Verona Love's Labour's Lost	Henry VI, part 1 Henry VI, part 2 Henry VI, part 3 Richard III King John	Titus Andronicus	Venus and Adonis Rape of Lucrece
II 1599	Midsummer Night's Dream Merchant of Venice Merry Wives of Windsor Much Ado About Nothing As You Like It	Richard II Henry IV, part 1 Henry IV, part 2 Henry V	Romeo and Juliet	Sonnets
III 1608	Twelfth Night Troilus and Cressida Measure for Measure All's Well That Ends Well		Julius Caesar Hamlet Othello Timon of Athens King Lear Macbeth Antony and Cleopatra Coriolanus	
IV 1613	Pericles Cymbeline A Winter's Tale The Tempest	Henry VIII		